Issues in Coursebook Evaluation

Critical New Literacies: The Praxis of English Language Teaching and Learning (PELT)

Series Editors

Marcelle Cacciattolo (*Victoria University, Australia*)
Tarquam McKenna (*Victoria University, Australia*)
Shirley Steinberg (*University of Calgary, Canada*)
Mark Vicars (*Victoria University, Australia*)

VOLUME 8

The titles published in this series are listed at *brill.com/cnli*

Issues in Coursebook Evaluation

Edited by

Maryam Azarnoosh, Mitra Zeraatpishe,
Akram Faravani and Hamid Reza Kargozari

BRILL
SENSE

LEIDEN | BOSTON

All chapters in this book have undergone peer review.

Library of Congress Cataloging-in-Publication Data

Names: Azarnoosh, Maryam, editor. | Zeraatpishe, Mitra, editor. | Faravani, Akram, editor. | Kargozari, Hamid Reza, editor.
Title: Issues in coursebook evaluation / Edited by Maryam Azarnoosh, Mitra Zeraatpishe, Akram Faravani and Hamid Reza Kargozari.
Description: Leiden, The Netherlands ; Boston : Brill Sense, [2018] | Series: Critical new literacies : the praxis of English language teaching and learning (PELT), ISSN 2542-9396 ; volume 8 | Includes bibliographical references and index.
Identifiers: LCCN 2018037083 (print) | LCCN 2018038654 (ebook) | ISBN 9789004387379 (E-book) | ISBN 9789004387355 (pbk. : alk. paper) | ISBN 9789004387362 (hardback)
Subjects: LCSH: English language--Textbooks for foreign speakers--Evaluation. | English language--Study and teaching--Foreign speakers.
Classification: LCC PE1128.A2 (ebook) | LCC PE1128.A2 I825 2018 (print) | DDC
    428.2/4029--dc23
LC record available at https://lccn.loc.gov/2018037083

ISSN 2542-9396
ISBN 978-90-04-38735-5 (paperback)
ISBN 978-90-04-38736-2 (hardback)
ISBN 978-90-04-38737-9 (e-book)

Copyright 2018 by Koninklijke Brill NV, Leiden, The Netherlands.
Koninklijke Brill NV incorporates the imprints Brill, Brill Hes & De Graaf, Brill Nijhoff, Brill Rodopi, Brill Sense and Hotei Publishing.
All rights reserved. No part of this publication may be reproduced, translated, stored in a retrieval system, or transmitted in any form or by any means, electronic, mechanical, photocopying, recording or otherwise, without prior written permission from the publisher.
Authorization to photocopy items for internal or personal use is granted by Koninklijke Brill NV provided that the appropriate fees are paid directly to The Copyright Clearance Center, 222 Rosewood Drive, Suite 910, Danvers, MA 01923, USA. Fees are subject to change.

This book is printed on acid-free paper and produced in a sustainable manner.

CONTENTS

Preface		vii
List of Figures and Tables		xi
1.	WH Questions in Book Evaluation: Why, How, When, and Who? *Vahid Nimehchisalem*	1
2.	Learners' Needs in Materials Evaluation *Saleh Al-Busaidi*	11
3.	Evaluating Language and Content in Coursebooks *Darío Luis Banegas*	21
4.	Evaluating Teaching Aids *Thom Kiddle*	31
5.	Assessing Intercultural Communicative Competence: Towards an Intercultural Approach to Language Teaching and Evaluation *Carlos Rico-Troncoso*	41
6.	Socio-Cultural Perspectives on Coursebook Evaluation *Martin Cortazzi and Lixian Jin*	65
7.	Conversation Analysis Criteria for Evaluating the Authenticity of ESL Textbook Conversations *Lilia Savova*	85
8.	Evaluation of ESP Textbooks *Maryam Azarnoosh, Mahboobeh Khosrojerdi and Mitra Zeraatpishe*	95
9.	E-textbook Evaluation Criteria Revisited *Hamid Reza Kargozari, Golnaz Peyvandi and Akram Faravani*	111
10.	Insightful Gains from Research on ELT Materials Evaluation *Jayakaran Mukundan, Seyed Ali Rezvani Kalajahi and Abdolvahed Zarifi*	121
About the Contributors		131
Index		135

PREFACE

The early ideas of developing a book on coursebook evaluation occurred during the 11th International TELLSI Conference held in Mashhad, Iran in 2013. After participating lectures, presentation sessions and panel discussions, we got into a hot debate on university courses, needs of EFL students, materials and recourses, etc. which finally led us to the decision we made on developing a book series on Issues in TEFL with volumes focusing on topics such as materials development and evaluation, SLA theories, syllabus designing and curriculum development to investigate contemporary aspects of teaching and learning English applicable in second/foreign language contexts.

Issues in Coursebook Evaluation takes a theory to practice approach with emphasis on theoretical underpinnings that lead into practical aspects of the process of textbook evaluation. The book covers the fundamental concepts in coursebook evaluation in reader-friendly chapters that make it easier for readers in the field to follow the main aspects of materials and textbook evaluation. Moreover, these review chapters reflect the voice and style of contributors in covering the issues and presenting scholarly ideas which turn this work to a valuable resource book in applied linguistics. This book not only serves as a potential basis for post-graduate courses on textbook evaluation or for research work, but also provides a practical guide for those interested in materials evaluation such as language teachers, academics, practitioners, and researchers. The outstanding point about this book is that there seems to be very few publications specifically devoted to coursebook evaluation. This has probably been due to the close relationship between materials development and evaluation and sometimes viewing them as the two sides of the same coin which has led to covering related issues mainly in books on materials development.

Coursebooks are indispensable parts of language learning programs and their careful selection in meeting the requirements of the courses along with the interaction of various other elements can lead to the success of the programs. This will not be possible unless a systematic and objective evaluation of textbooks is conducted based on informed principles of language learning and teaching, needs of the learners, goals of the course, learning outcomes, and several other interrelated factors. In an EFL context in which the coursebooks may be the only source of language learning, the evaluation of textbooks to adopt or adapt them seem to gain prominence. That is why this book specifically focuses of coursebook evaluation in EFL and ESL contexts to pull together the theory and practice of materials evaluation and to illustrate some viewpoints and insights which can inform language teachers, practitioners, textbook and materials evaluators on issues of current concern. The central themes in evaluating coursebooks, in this book, are presented as outlined below.

PREFACE

In the first chapter, Nimehchisalem expresses that among English language teaching materials, books are of particular significance and have been used as an inseparable component of most language classes for ages. This is particularly true for EFL contexts in which learners are less likely to be exposed to authentic examples of the English language. This underlines the significance of books in EFL settings, and in turn accentuates their evaluation. Accordingly, Nimehchisalem addresses some fundamental questions that have engaged experts in the area of ELT learning-teaching materials evaluation for years. Specifically, he focuses on these four questions: (1) Why should anyone bother about book evaluation? (2) How is it possible to evaluate books? (3) When should books be evaluated? And (4) Who should be in charge of book evaluation?

In Chapter 2, Al-Busaidi emphasizes on the significance of needs analysis by stating that it is a forgotten aspect of materials evaluation. He defines needs and explains the needs analysis process. He also discusses the main concerns in needs analysis, the procedure of identifying needs, different types of tools to collect information, and how to interpret and analyze the data. In the third chapter on evaluating language and content in coursebooks, Banegas considers Content and Language Integrated Learning (CLIL) in EFL contexts. He first specifies why teachers should evaluate textbooks. Then he offers a brief outline of CLIL and how it may appear in coursebooks. Finally, he suggests how teachers can decide about adopting a coursebook under a CLIL framework. This chapter is followed by Thom Kiddle's exploration of approaches to evaluation of physical teaching aids, designed primarily for language teaching and learning in Chapter 4. He also considers the evaluation of digital tools which are not explicitly designed for educational purposes but may be used in classroom teaching, or in teacher-supported individual or collaborative learning.

Considering the purpose of language learning which is communication, in Chapter 5, Troncoso reflects on the significance of the new trends of the communicative approach for language teaching, specifically the importance of the intercultural approach for language education and how it can be assessed in communicative activities. He provides some key elements to take into account when evaluating, adapting or developing activities for Intercultural Communicative Competence (ICC). He also provides examples of some communicative activities proposed in an adapted Spanish Unit. Closely related to this topic, Chapter 6 deals with socio-cultural perspectives in evaluating coursebooks. In this comprehensive chapter, Cortazzi and Jin discuss socio-cultural issues and basic evaluation criteria to be considered when evaluating TEFL coursebooks. They indicate a range of complexities that make this evaluation difficult when both global and local pedagogic considerations are not taken into account. They also emphasize on reflexivity which is a kind of meta-reflection about one's socio-cultural orientation and expectations within TEFL which provides teachers and learners with global and local social and cultural awareness. They end this chapter with evaluating socio-cultural aspects of some TEFL coursebooks of students in China.

PREFACE

While the first six chapters deal with coursebook evaluation in general, in Chapter 7, Savova focuses only on a specific aspect that is ESL textbook conversations and investigates the criteria used to evaluate their authenticity. As she states, language learners find textbook conversations different from real-life conversations since they lack authenticity and regardless of attempts made to change this situation still some artificiality in ESL textbook and classroom conversations can be observed. To deal with this issue, she first analyzes sample textbook conversations, then demonstrates that both linguistic analysis and conversation analysis (CA) can provide conversational criteria to evaluate the authenticity of textbook conversations. She introduces CA as a tool to analyze real-life conversations and applies it in a sample ESL textbook conversation. At the end, she offers some criteria for evaluating the authenticity of textbook conversations.

Considering the fact that language learners have different purposes in studying English, in Chapter 8, Azarnoosh, Khosrojerdi, and Zeraatpishe review the main issues in ESP textbook evaluation. After mentioning the importance of textbook evaluation and conducting needs analysis in evaluating ESP materials, they discuss some proposed language learning and teaching principles in developing coursebooks which underlie ESP textbook evaluation. In addition, the specificity of ESP context and its features are discussed. Taking these aspects into consideration, the authors elaborate on ESP evaluation criteria and methods of conducting it.

Chapter 9 deals with e-textbook evaluation. In this chapter, Kargozari, Peyvandi, and Faravani point to the fact that the textbook market is revolutionized by the digital age which means availability of e-textbooks, and consequently the need to evaluate such materials. To select the most appropriate e-textbooks, they recommend evaluation of e-textbooks to find their potential strengths and weaknesses. So they elaborate on definitions of e-books, their advantages, and review the criteria required for evaluating e-textbooks.

The book ends with Chapter 10 on insightful gains from research on ELT materials evaluation. In this chapter, Mukundan, Rezvani Kalajahi and Zarifi discuss the advantages of research on materials evaluation considering the following two aspects: (1) the main areas of research in ELT materials evaluation, and (2) the benefit and impact of ELT materials research on teachers and teaching-learning. Concerning the first aspect, they point to the development of evaluation instruments, evaluation of teaching materials, and emergence of the composite framework. The second issue deals with benefits of materials research on textbooks, learner needs, and teacher professional development. The concluding remark is that still more work and research needs to be done in the area of textbook evaluation.

We hope that this book will be considered as a valuable contribution to the applied linguistics and English language teaching field. We also hope you enjoy reading this book and find it applicable when evaluating language learning coursebooks. At the end, we express our sincere appreciation to all the authors of this volume without whom this book would have never come to life, Atefeh Quds who set the format of the chapters, and the reviewers and editors at Brill | Sense.

FIGURES AND TABLES

FIGURES

5.1.	Dimensions and components of ICC	42
5.2.	Competences for language teaching and learning	45
6.1.	Some perceptions of culture which from a global perspective are misaligned for representing 'target' cultures in TEFL coursebooks	67
6.2.	Some disciplinary perspectives giving conceptions of socio-cultural language use	68
6.3.	Some stages of evaluation of socio-cultural aspects of TEFL materials	73
6.4.	Developing cultural comparison, reflexivity and identity through parallel culture focus sections of cultural readers	76
6.5.	Socio-cultural features observable in unit tasks for student activities	77
6.6.	Examples of activities to develop creativity in social contexts in pairs and groups for classroom presentations	79
6.7.	Raising awareness of politeness practices across culture	79
6.8.	Three stages of participation activities to develop reflexivity in intercultural communication skills	80
10.1.	The composite framework for textbook evaluation	126
10.2.	The total number of tokens in textbook 1 (FB) and textbook 2 (SM)	128

TABLES

2.1.	Steps of needs analysis	15
2.2.	Needs analysis instruments and audience in different situations	17
5.1.	Competences for teaching, learning and evaluation	45
5.2.	Criteria to assess ICC within communicative tasks	50
7.1.	Criteria for evaluating ESL conversation authenticity	92
10.1.	Difficulty analysis of items in the SEC	123
10.2.	Summary of the statistics of textbook 1 (FB) and textbook 2 (SM)	128

VAHID NIMEHCHISALEM

1. WH QUESTIONS IN BOOK EVALUATION

Why, How, When, and Who?

INTRODUCTION

Among other English Language Teaching (ELT) materials, which cover an extensive range from English language learning software to videos, books have been traditionally of particular significance. The term book, in this chapter, is interchangeably used for both the ELT coursebook (which covers the whole package including a student book, workbook, and teacher's guide) and the ELT textbook (which refers to the core book covering all or most of the topics in a course). Books are materials that have been used in English language classrooms for ages since they help the teacher equally emphasize the syllabus to be covered during a course. Using books for teaching languages has been harshly criticized by Sheldon (1988), who refers to them as necessary evil, and Brumfit (1980), who argues that they are skillfully marketed rubbish. Albeit with such criticisms, the book seems to be an inseparable component of most language classes. This is particularly true for English as a Foreign Language (EFL) situation. EFL learners, unlike those in English as a Second Language (ESL) setting, are less likely to be exposed to authentic examples of the English language. This underlines the significance of books in EFL settings, and in turn accentuates the importance of their evaluation.

The present chapter will address some fundamental questions that have engaged experts in the area of ELT learning-teaching material evaluation for years. More specifically, these questions will be:

1. Why should anyone bother about book evaluation?
2. How is it possible to evaluate books?
3. When should books be evaluated?
4. Who should be in charge of book evaluation?

The chapter aims to answer each of these questions, respectively.

WHY BOOK EVALUATION?

The primary question that comes to mind is the rationale behind evaluating ELT books. Based on Sheldon (1988), there are two main reasons for ELT book evaluation. First, it can help program developers, syllabus designers, and language instructors select the best possible book for the learners in their present educational setting. A book selected in *ad hoc* manner may not match with the learners' needs and interests. Such practice will certainly have negative impacts on their learning outcome. By contrast, informed decisions that are made based on systematic and objective evaluation of the book will secure the match between the students' needs and the objectives of the book.

In addition to the fact that evaluation helps in selection of suitable books, it also provides useful information for curriculum writers who wish to make adaptations to less successful parts of the selected book. It is almost impossible to find a book that perfectly suits the learners' needs. Therefore, curriculum designers will often find themselves obliged to make changes to its content or activities. Book evaluation results help them diagnose any problematic section in the book while it is being taught. Once these parts have been detected, they are discarded from the course outline. Similarly, course instructors benefit from evaluating books, which shows the merits and demerits of the books they are using. An awareness of the possible strengths and weaknesses of the books enables teachers to replace the less successful parts with more useful and suitable content and tasks. This creates an opportunity for instructors to improve the teaching quality and learning outcome of their future instruction.

Failing to evaluate or misevaluate books will have serious but silent consequences which may be why we normally choose to turn a blind eye to book evaluation reports. In traditional educational systems, ELT books are developed by the Ministry of Education and mandated to be used at schools. In such systems, even when the books do not prove useful, most teachers will simply continue teaching them because they are given no other choice than covering the entire syllabus and preparing their class for an examination. In less radical settings, the teacher may be allowed to use alternative materials to replace the book prescribed by the Ministry. In these systems, few people usually complain since the general assumption is that the book is provided for 'free'. However, it should be noted that any state-sponsored textbook has its own hidden costs (Mukundan, 2003).

HOW TO EVALUATE BOOKS?

Methods of book evaluation vary. Five different ways will be discussed here, including impressionistic evaluation, scale-based evaluation, teacher logs, software packages, and composite frameworks.

Impressionistic Evaluation

This form of evaluation relies on evaluators' intuitional decision about the usefulness of the book. The evaluator looks into some pages while flipping through others and making holistic judgments on the usefulness of the book. This form of evaluation extensively relies on the evaluator's experience and expertise. Novice practitioners find it challenging to make reliable judgments impressionistically. The reason is that they still need some time to gain experience and develop the implicit set of criteria based on which they can make good decisions. Impressionistic evaluation is cost-effective and takes a relatively short time, but its main shortcoming is its high subjectivity which puts the reliability of its outcome at risk.

Scale-Based Evaluation

Scale-based evaluation provides a set of evaluative criteria in the form of a checklist, based on which the evaluator examines the most crucial features of a book. The result of such evaluation will often be valid if the checklist is developed and rigorously tested for its validity. It will also result in a reliable decision if the evaluator has sufficient experience. The outcome of scale-based book evaluation is commonly more explicit, sophisticated, and comprehensive than that of impressionistic evaluation that is implicit and intuitive. Checklists commonly focus on the most significant domains to be considered in evaluating ELT books. The outcome therefore usually covers most of the constructs related to the issue of ELT book evaluation. A lot of ELT book evaluation checklists are available in the literature (e.g., Cunningsworth, 1995; Harmer, 1991; Ur, 1996). These checklists help language instructors and evaluators examine important features of the selected book, features like physical attributes, aims, layout, methodology, organization, presentation of language skills (i.e., speaking, listening, reading, and writing), language sub-skills (grammar, vocabulary, etc.), and language functions, among others.

Depending on the data its items elicit, a checklist can be placed in either side of a continuum with qualitative checklists on one side and quantitative checklists on the other. Qualitative checklists have open-ended items. Richards (2001) developed a checklist that can be considered a qualitative checklist since the evaluator using it will have to provide subjective responses to the questions that it puts forth. In contrast, Skierso's (1991) checklist is quantitative since it gets the evaluator to assign 0 to 4, signifying 'totally lacking' to 'excellent' for the book being examined. The Likert style scale of a quantitative scale allows the evaluator to measure the suitability of the book under evaluation. It is also possible to have a checklist that represents a combination of qualitative and quantitative items. For instance, Sheldon's (1988) checklist begins with a part on 'Factual details' of the book under examination. The part is followed by a section on 'Assessment' of the quality of different features of the book (such as 'authenticity' and 'flexibility') that is rated, 'poor', 'fair', 'good', or 'excellent'. Finally, the checklist ends with a section with questions like 'To what extent has the book realized its stated objectives?'

Each type of book evaluation checklist has its own merits or demerits. Qualitative checklists will naturally result in more in-depth examination of the book while quantitative checklists may turn out to be more convenient and reliable. Mukundan and Ahour (2010) present an overview of textbook evaluation checklists developed from 1970 to 2008. They review over 40 checklists, divided into qualitative and quantitative categories.

Checklists are useful instruments, but it is easy to develop an unreliable and invalid checklist. Many checklists are available in the literature without any empirical proof of their construct validity. Even when they are validated, some of them lack practicality. For example, there are items in some checklists that seek to elicit information on the load and distribution of the new vocabulary items. Obviously, it is very difficult to provide accurate information on how many times a word appears throughout a book unless the book comes with an accurate index or unless some specialized software is used. Related to the issue of practicality is economy. Some checklists are too long. Skierso's (1991) checklist, for example, exceeds 4000 running words and contains many domains. This may contribute to its construct validity but undermines its economy. Another disadvantage of some checklists is the use of technical jargon which may sound vague for the novice evaluator. To offer an example, in the vocabulary section of some of the available checklists (such as Mukundan & Nimehchisalem, 2012), the term 'recycle' may confuse some evaluators. Rephrasing the term in a way that inexperienced evaluators would find it more comprehensible (i.e., 'repeat' instead of 'recycle') would facilitate working with the instrument. A final noteworthy point which is often ignored in the development of some checklists is the methodological principles of instrument development. As an example, when a single item measures more than one dimension and violates the principle of unidimensionality, it can confuse the rater and reduce reliability of its outcome.

Reflective Logs

Reflective or teaching logs provide another option for evaluating ELT books. Teachers may keep logs either in a structured or an unstructured way. Structured logs are easier to work with since they provide a list of questions for the teacher to reflect upon, questions like:

1. Which part(s) of the book was effective?
2. What part(s) can be adapted and improved in future classes?
3. What were the students' reactions to the lesson presented by the book?

On the other hand, teachers may keep a journal-like unstructured log on how the book works in the real class situation. Unstructured logs do not limit the scope of evaluation, leaving the teacher free to evaluate a book as it works. This sometimes results in more creative and natural evaluation on the part of the teacher, and if shared with the book authors or publishers, it provides them with more original feedback on what needs to be changed in the next editions.

Despite the useful information they can provide, teacher logs are not very popular among teachers. Keeping a log is an added task to language teachers' heavy schedule. Therefore, some teachers may refrain from keeping a log, and in cases it is mandatory, some teachers do not take it seriously and just dumb it down. In addition, some teachers may not find it easy to write about the way a book works. There may also be a lot of redundant information in a log which makes its analysis taxing. Finally, teacher logs are highly subjective which reduces the generalizability of their outcome. Therefore, some curriculum evaluators may find field notes compiled by an expert who impartially observed the class while the book was being taught more reliable sources of feedback and a better alternative for teacher logs.

Software Packages

In recent years, computers have enabled book evaluators to examine the load and distribution of vocabulary items presented by ELT books quickly and accurately. Software packages like Concordance, EZText, HAMLET, HyperResearch, MicroConcrd, and MonoConc Pro, TextQuest, WordNet, and WordSmith can be used to find useful information on the words used in a book, such as:

1. Total number of running words (tokens),
2. Total number of different words (types),
3. List of all the words in alphabetical order or ordered based on their frequency, and
4. Concordance listing of a word, which shows a selected word as it was used in the book with five words before and five words after it.

Research on ELT book evaluation using computer software prevails. These studies focus on the presentation of varying vocabulary or grammatical items presented in ELT books, to name but a few, articles (Mukundan, Leong, & Nimehchisalem, 2012), modal auxiliary verbs (Khojasteh, 2012), prepositions (Norwati, 2013), and phrasal verbs (Zarifi, 2013).

Software like WordSmith offers a unique method to investigate how well a word has been presented and repeated in a book, but this provides a narrow worm-view of the suitability of a book. The overall suitability of a book cannot be based on the outcome of such studies. Another shortcoming of this method of ELT book evaluation is that it fails to study the book as it works in the real classroom setting. Finally, in some cases, analysis may be demanding. Software can help only when the book is available in text-file format. Otherwise, the book has to be scanned, converted to text-file format, and edited before analysis.

Composite Frameworks

A composite framework of ELT book evaluation integrates two or more methods to evaluate the suitability of an ELT book (Mukundan, 2009). A good example is Retrotext-E (Mukundan, 2010), which enables an evaluation of:

1. Word loading and distribution patterns,
2. Checklist evaluation, and
3. Teacher log

The first function of the software enables the evaluator to obtain an overall frequency count and distribution patterns of all the words in the book much in the same way as WordSmith. It can also show to what extent the words in the book and/or each of its chapters corresponds with those in a reference word list such as the General Service List (West, 1953) or Academic Word List (Coxhead, 2000). In this way, the evaluator can tell how adequately the book presents the essential vocabulary to the target audience. The software also comes with a Likert style quantitative checklist that the teacher can use after each lesson to evaluate the usefulness of that particular lesson in a more systematic and objective manner. Finally, the Teacher log function allows teachers to type and save their reflective logs and view other teachers' logs who have also used Retrotext-E to keep their own logs and who wish to share them with their colleagues. Thus, apart from its composite ELT book evaluation framework, a unique feature of Retrotext-E is that it can save and compile all the evaluations made by different teachers. These evaluations can all be reviewed later by a program evaluator, publisher, author, or researcher who is interested in more than one teachers' evaluation of the same ELT book as it worked in their classes. The shortcoming of the software is that it cannot be downloaded online yet, a feature that its future versions are expected to have.

WHEN TO EVALUATE BOOKS?

It is possible to evaluate books before they are used, while they are being used, as well as after they have been used, depending on the purpose of their evaluation (Cunningsworth, 1995; Ellis, 1997). Pre-use evaluation is appropriate for predictive purposes. When a syllabus designer is looking for a book that best suits the needs of the students in their target teaching situation, s/he needs to evaluate several books before they have been actually used. A systematic prognostic evaluation of the available books results in more informed decisions particularly when it is conducted by a team of experienced evaluators who are aware of the target students' needs and interests as well as the target teachers' preferences. Unfortunately, predictive evaluation is totally ignored in traditional top-down educational systems where the book is developed by government-sponsored publishers and prescribed to be used all over the country. This invariably results in poor learning quality on the part of the student whose needs and interests are often neglected while developing the book.

Sometimes program evaluators need to assess the usefulness of a book that has been recently selected to be used in their present teaching situation. This type of assessment, which is called in-use or progressive evaluation, will help the program evaluator observe the way in which the book is used by a teacher in real language classroom setting and find out the strengths and weaknesses of the book. This form of evaluation often results in valuable findings that can be used for making adaptations for certain parts of the book which were not really suitable for the students. These changes are observed in future classes and may be revised or may replace the original part in the book. This type of evaluation is formative in nature and allows an on-going assessment of each lesson and activity as they are taught throughout the course. In-use evaluation is very valuable but it is also time-consuming and can be costly. This type of evaluation is common in developed countries in which built-in syllabus design procedures are followed (Ellis, 1993). In such learning-teaching contexts syllabus designers adapt the syllabus to the way in which students tend to learn the language (Brumfit, 1981). Hence, in order to fulfill the syllabus objectives, teachers are free to select from a bank of books or materials suggested by the Ministry or to develop their own activities and materials. This makes it crucial to evaluate teacher-developed materials progressively in order to diagnose any probable shortcoming and to ensure that their course is in line with the determined syllabus objectives.

Finally, at times ELT books may be evaluated after they have been used for retrospective purposes. Post-use evaluation gives the evaluator an overall picture of the way a book worked or failed to work in a given learning-teaching situation. Based on the findings of such evaluation, ground rules are set for developing similar materials in the future.

WHO SHOULD EVALUATE BOOKS?

Book evaluation can be a very complicated and demanding task with long-lasting effects. ELT books have many stakeholders who are usually denied the right of being able to voice their needs and interests. The person that seems to be the best candidate to evaluate an ELT book is the teacher who is using it. However, it should be noted that the teacher should have the adequate expertise and experience to provide a valid and reliable evaluation of the book. Apart from these, it should be noted that teaching is a low-paid and highly demanding job with heavy workload. Experienced teachers are usually busier and having to evaluate a book may be the last straw. Therefore, it is equally important to consider that the teacher is given sufficient time with extendable deadlines to evaluate a book.

Determining who should evaluate books is a very tricky decision to make particularly in situations where textbooks are prescribed by the State. If the same state-sponsored publisher that developed the book is demanded to evaluate it, the results will definitely be biased. Even if the best instrument is used, the evaluation outcome will be far from reliable. Therefore, it may be argued that the best person who can evaluate ELT books is an impartial expert that is also an experienced teacher trained for this purpose. However, the question in such situations is whether this individual is familiar with *all* the students' needs and interests as well as *all* the teachers' preferences.

CONCLUSION

This chapter has discussed four basic questions in ELT book evaluation. First the reason behind ELT book evaluation was discussed. As it can be concluded, book evaluation is essential because it (1) helps curriculum developers select the right book for a given group of students, (2) aids them to eliminate and adapt the unsuitable parts in the book, which consequently (3) saves a lot of unnecessary hidden costs. In addition to these, the most remarkable reason for book evaluation is that it results in improved learner engagement and learning outcome. When a book is chosen meticulously as a result of rigorous evaluation and when it is progressively assessed for its usefulness, the instructor will take the course more seriously and the student will find it more engaging and learn better.

Next, the different possible ways for book evaluation were discussed. Books are frequently evaluated impressionistically based on the evaluator's implicit criteria. The outcome is often something very subjective. Even when the judgment is based on an instrument, one cannot claim that one's evaluation is completely objective. This brings about issues of validity and reliability. There are methods to improve the relevance (validity) and consistency (reliability) of the evaluation. However, whether in reality these methods are followed to enhance the outcome makes an enormous difference.

It was also noted that evaluation works best when it starts before, while, and after its use. This means that book evaluation is often not the one-shot summative type as it is commonly perceived. Rather, it has to be on-going and formative if it is meant to yield some concrete dependable outcome. This sounds very easy, but in practice, it is usually avoided since it costs time, money, and energy to evaluate a book in this way.

Finally, the question of who should evaluate books was discussed. As mentioned, numerous stakeholders may be involved in ELT book evaluation. The most important stakeholders would be the learners whose needs must not be neglected; otherwise, the selected book will not be learner-centered. As another group of stakeholders, teachers usually look for books that are comprehensive, including a teacher's guide among other support materials, such as online test banks with answer keys. The other group would be those in charge of covering the costs that could be the students themselves, their guardians, their school, or the government. Publishers should also be in the picture; otherwise, there will be no material available at all to be evaluated. As it was concluded, the best person to evaluate a book would be an experienced impartial teacher who has been trained for the task.

Those who are involved in evaluating ELT materials usually find themselves tangled in a web of issues in their endeavor to make the right decision. In practice, book evaluation is not an easy and smooth task to undertake. It may bring about bitter consequences for some stakeholders who will choose to resist against change. In such situations, one may think ignorance is bliss. However, it will cause chronic irreparable damages to the educational system and ultimately to the society. When a book is selected based on invalid criteria, misperception of learners' needs, and incorrect assumption of the teacher's preferences, it will negatively influence the entire course. If managed efficiently, evaluation as it has been depicted in this chapter can be a turning point in the history of an unsuccessful educational system.

REFERENCES

Brumfit, C. J. (1980). Seven last slogans. *Modern Language Journal, 7*(1), 30–31.
Brumfit, C. J. (1981). The notional syllabus revisited. *Applied Linguistics, 2*(1), 83–89.
Coxhead, A. (2000). A new academic word list. *TESOL Quarterly, 34*(2), 213–238.
Cunningsworth, A. (1995). *Choosing your coursebook*. Oxford: Heinemann.
Ellis, R. (1997). *SLA research and language teaching*. Oxford: Oxford University Press.
Harmer, J. (1991). *The practice of English language teaching*. Harlow: Longman.
Khojasteh, L. (2011). *A corpus-based study of modal auxiliary verbs used in the Malaysian English language textbooks* (Unpublished doctoral dissertation). Universiti Putra Malaysia (UPM), Serdang, Malaysia.
Mukundan, J. (2003). State-sponsored textbooks: Are there hidden costs in these "free" books? *The English Teacher: An International Journal of the Assumption University, Bangkok, Thailand, 6*(2), 133–143.
Mukundan, J. (2009). *ESL textbook evaluation: A composite framework*. Köln: Lambert Academic Publishing.
Mukundan, J. (2010). Retrotext-E 1.0: The beginnings of computer-based ELT textbook evaluation. *Advances in Language and Literary Studies, 1*(2), 270–280.
Mukundan, J., & Ahour, T. (2010). A review of textbook evaluation checklists across four decades (1970–2008). In B. Tomlinson & H. Masuhara (Eds.), *Research for materials development in language learning* (pp. 336–352). London: Continuum International Publishing Group.
Mukundan, J., Leong, A., & Nimehchisalem, V. (2012). Distribution of articles in Malaysian secondary school English language textbooks. *English Language and Literature Studies, 2*(2), 62–70.
Mukundan, J., & Nimehchisalem, V. (2012). Evaluative criteria of an English language textbook evaluation checklist. *Journal of Language Teaching Research, 3*(6), 1128–1134.
Richards, J. C. (2001). *Curriculum development in language teaching*. Cambridge: Cambridge University Press.
Roslim, N. (2013). *A corpus-based analysis of prepositions used in the English language textbooks* (Unpublished doctoral dissertation). Universiti Putra Malaysia (UPM), Serdang, Malaysia.
Sheldon, L. E. (1988). Evaluating ELT textbooks and materials. *ELT Journal, 42*(4), 237–246.
Skierso, A. (1991). Textbook selection and evaluation. In M. Celce-Murcia (Ed.), *Teaching English as a second or foreign language* (2nd ed., pp. 432–453). Boston, MA: Heinle & Heinle Publishers.
Ur, P. (1996). *A course in language teaching: Practice and theory*. Cambridge: Cambridge University Press.
West, M. (1953). *A general service list of English words*. London: Longman, Green and Co.
Zarifi, V. (2013). *A corpus-based study of phrasal verbs in Malaysian ESL secondary school textbooks*. (Unpublished doctoral dissertation). Universiti Putra Malaysia (UPM), Serdang, Malaysia.

Vahid Nimehchisalem
Faculty of Modern Languages and Communication
Universiti Putra Malaysia
Malaysia

SALEH AL-BUSAIDI

2. LEARNERS' NEEDS IN MATERIALS EVALUATION

INTRODUCTION

Materials and especially commercial textbooks often form the basis for learning and teaching. In EFL settings, textbooks are the main source of contact with the foreign language (Hamid et al., 2016). Materials evaluation can be a complex and sometimes daunting task. Evaluators often develop or use criteria in the form of checklists to guide their judgment. These checklists vary in their coverage from physical features of the textbook to its underlying principles of teaching and learning. The intended outcome from such an exercise is to identify the material that closely matches the requirements of the target situation. The literature is replete with checklists (see for example, Cunningworth, 1995; Daoud & Celce-Murcia, 1979; Mukundan & Nimehchisalem, 2012; Skiero, 1991). However, what is noticed about such checklists is that they are differently informed and motivated (Roberts, 1996). Also, they tend to be generic and program centered. They do not take into account the specific needs of the learners who are the end users of such materials and their perspective should therefore be central to the selection process. Learners become more motivated to learn the language if it is presented to them in material that is relevant to their needs and culture (Tajeddin & Teimournezhad, 2015). As is widely known, commercial materials are not written to serve a particular group of learners. Their needs have to be clearly defined. Needs generally refer to the gap between the current state and the desired state. They can take the form of knowledge, skills or attitudes to be acquired. Needs analysis is the process of identifying the gap between the existing skills and knowledge and those that are needed for the target language use. It seeks information on different types of information. First, it identifies the situations in which the language will be used. Second, it describes the purposes for which the language is needed. It also specifies the type and register of communication where the target language will be used, that is, written, spoken, formal, informal, online, and offline. Finally, needs analysis determines the level of proficiency that will be required. Materials evaluators should remember that the assessment of learners' needs is not straightforward and therefore it requires eliciting information from multiple sources. Information from needs analysis is used to determine the course goals and content. It is crucial that needs analysis is conducted efficiently and carefully.

This chapter describes the needs analysis phase, which the author strongly argues should precede or at least accompany the materials evaluation phase. It is only after we have established a firm understanding of the needs of the target learners that we are able to find the most suitable materials. In many cases of materials evaluation, learners' needs are often oversimplified, and learners' perspectives are often overlooked. Materials are normally selected in relation to program objectives which may and may not necessarily reflect the true learners' needs, and other logistical considerations. Alternatively, materials are evaluated based on readymade generic checklist which are not designed for a particular group of learners (Sheldon, 1988).

WHAT ARE NEEDS?

The term 'need' refers to the gap between 'what is' and 'what should be' (Witkin et al., 1995), or the gap between 'real' and 'ideal' (Reviere et al., 1996). In other words, needs are concerned with the future, or what should happen, rather than with what used to happen or what is happening at present (Titcomb, 2000). Researchers have drawn distinctions between the term 'need' and other related terms. Hutchinson and Waters (1987) distinguish between target needs (what learners need to do in the target situation) and learning needs (what learners need to do in order to learn). Nation and Macalister (2010) divide needs into three types: necessities (what is necessary in the learners' use of the target language), lacks (what learners lack from previous training or education), and wants (what learners wish to learn). A distinction is also made between 'subjective' needs versus 'objective' needs. The former refer to the needs as perceived by learners themselves, whereas the latter refer to needs as determined by objective means such as tests. Subjective needs are identified through self-assessment tools where learners decide about their current state and where they want to be. This division of needs into different types helps understand them and helps materials evaluators in their review work. It helps materials evaluators prioritize the course focus and fit it within the time limit.

WHAT IS NEEDS ANALYSIS?

The process that is followed to identify learner needs is often referred to as 'needs analysis'. Other terms used are 'needs assessment' and 'situation analysis'. These terms are often used interchangeably. Nation and Macalister (2010) differentiate between needs analysis and environment analysis. Needs analysis refers to the learners' needs of the target language, whereas environment analysis refers to the situational factors that affect decisions about the course. Examples of the situational factors include time factor, teachers' background and education and resources. In this chapter, I will use the term 'needs analysis' for the sake of consistency to cover all elements related to learners' needs and situational constraints.

Needs analysis determines the gaps between the current ability and the desired ability. The rationale behind needs analysis is that each learner and learning situation is unique and has their own purposes for learning a particular language. The concept 'needs analysis' is also used in industry and business. This stage is considered the most laborious, yet most important, aspect of materials evaluation. However, this is one of the fundamental phases as it lays the ground for all subsequent work in the process.

There are benefits in conducting needs analysis. First, it shows learners the relevance of what they are learning to their needs and interests. Learners, especially adults, are likely to be more engaged when they see the importance and relevance of what they are learning. Second, needs analysis helps learners identify where they are in terms of knowledge, skills and competencies and where they wish to be. Needs analysis is used to discover leaner needs and present them into meaningful units that can be used to create learning goals and objectives and subsequently develop or evaluate materials. There is no best way to identify learners' needs. People follow different procedures and use different means of establishing needs. The decision about which way to use depends on the scope, resources and constraints. However, in many cases, materials evaluators and teachers inevitably rely, at least partially, on their prior knowledge and experience about what learners need. While learning situations share many characteristics, each situation has its own requirements, constraints and resources.

Answers to the questions in the needs analysis should lead to decisions about the different aspects materials evaluators should pay attention to when reviewing materials. Depending on how extensive and detailed the needs analysis is, the information gleaned from this procedure will vary. The next section discusses some fundamental considerations in conducting needs analysis.

KEY CONSIDERATIONS IN NEEDS ANALYSIS

There are some important points that materials evaluators should consider when conducting needs analysis. One important fact to realize about needs analysis is that it is an ongoing process. There are two aspects to this. First, it is not always possible to conduct needs analysis before the course takes place. Teachers may find themselves in situations where the course is already underway. In this case, teachers can find out about learners' needs. One way to do this is to ask learners to rate a list of statements that describe their learning preferences, course content, etc. (Nation & Macalister, 2010). Second, needs are not straightforward. Their identification and interpretation is based on the values and judgments of the different 'stakeholders'. It is therefore crucial that information about learner needs is elicited from various sources. Third, needs are dynamic in nature and they are likely to change after the initial needs analysis, depending on learner variables and environmental constraints. If the same course is offered to a different group of learners, there should ideally be another round of needs analysis conducted in order to identify the needs of the new students and determine the course elements that need to be modified. This will ensure that the course responds to the students' needs and interests. It is therefore necessary to repeat the needs analysis exercise and make it part of the material evaluation plan. This needs analysis does not have to be extensive.

Another important consideration is the relevance of the data gathered. This will be determined by the way information is gathered and the source of that information. Each learning situation consists of a number of stakeholders (i.e., individuals who benefit or are affected by the course). The materials evaluator should identify the 'key' stakeholders who should be targeted at the needs analysis stage. These data sources should be the ones who will give objective information about what is required. When learners realize that the course is arranged in a way that responds to their needs and interests they feel motivated to exert more effort in meeting its requirements.

A further important consideration is reliability and validity of the needs analysis tools. Needs are varied and they constantly change. They are also not straightforward. Therefore, it is important that needs analysis covers a wide range of perspectives and situations where the target language is used. It is important that learners' perspectives are sought and considered when new materials are evaluated. However, the reliability and validity of self-perceived student data should be checked. The complexity of needs analysis requires that tools used for data collection be reliable and valid (Nation & Macalister, 2010). Reliability and validity can be maximized through the use of varied and standardized instruments. Examples of standardized instruments include tests and observation checklists. The more sources of information are used the more reliable the data is likely to be. As for validity, the materials evaluator should ensure that the tools are relevant to the task and to the nature of the course. Again, this should be judged by experts and professionals other than those involved in the course. Nation and Macalister (2010) point out that in many cases logistics and practicality overrule validity and reliability but they stress that priority should always be given to validity.

When gathering information about learners' needs, we should distinguish between what learners 'want' and what they actually 'need'. It is the needs that should be given priority for instruction to have impact on learning. In some situations, learners may not be aware of what will make the best impact. For example, for a group of adult learners who need to learn English to write technical communication, they may want to be given ready-made formats and expressions instead of acquiring the skills of expressing meaning and communicating ideas using a variety of linguistic tools.

We should remember that if the new materials are intended to bring change to the learner either in terms of new knowledge, behavior or attitude, then the evaluation should be based on the learner's needs and interests. Judgments about course goals, objectives and content should not be based on the material evaluator's assumptions but rather on rigorous and systematic analysis of the learner's needs. Proper needs analysis leads to informed decisions about instructional intervention. Finally, information that is obtained from needs analysis must be relevant to and useful for the development of the course as a whole. Therefore, it is advisable to pilot the instrument first to measure its effectiveness and identify any potential factors that might affect the process of obtaining information about learn needs. The usefulness of a needs analysis depends on the type of data gathering techniques used.

HOW ARE NEEDS IDENTIFIED?

There is no one standardized, agreed upon procedure for conducting needs analysis, as it depends on the nature of the course, scope of work and the resources and constraints in each situation. However, researchers have offered some guiding steps that can help materials evaluators in their mission of investigating learners' needs. Table 2.1 summarizes these steps. This procedure assumes that needs analysis is a recursive process.

Table 2.1. Steps of needs analysis

No.	Step	Explanation
1	Identify the purpose and audience of the needs analysis.	Decide about who the stakeholders are.
2	Decide on the information to be gathered.	List the type of information you need to discover. Are you interested in the situations, tasks, topics, or skills?
3	Decide on the best way to gather information.	There are various instruments but the materials evaluator should choose the most suitable one(s).
4	Gather data.	Data can be gathered in notes, forms, audio or video recording.
5	Interpret data.	Find ways to make sense of the data. Data needs to be classified into meaningful chunks.
6	Act on data.	Use findings to make decisions about different aspects of the course that the materials should meet.
7	Evaluate the impact and effectiveness of the action.	Once the materials have been adopted and used, they should be evaluated in terms of relevance and impact.
8	Revise the course as needed or gather further information.	Based on feedback, the materials are adapted or replaced; or further data is gathered.

There are many ways materials evaluators can use to arrive at learners' needs. The decision about the best way to use depends primarily on the nature of the course and the context, and resources available. The different types of needs analysis tools include:

1. Interviews (individual or group)
2. Observations
3. Questionnaires

4. Tests (placement, diagnostic, achievement, proficiency)
5. Case studies (individual or group)
6. Diary studies
7. Records analysis
8. Text analysis (e.g. analysis of materials learners will need to comprehend)
9. Meetings/discussions
10. Systems analysis (analysis of organizational structures and decision making process)
11. Literature review (review of research findings on similar situations or needs)

Discovering needs involves identifying the situations where the target language will be used, the tasks that the learners need to perform and the linguistic knowledge required to function in these situations and tasks. Based on the context, the materials evaluator chooses the most suitable instrument that elicits spoken or written input from the learners. For example, learners may be asked to respond to a prompt or a set of questions. Alternatively, the materials evaluator may decide that it is important to observe learner behavior in action. Good needs analysis utilizes more than one tool for the sake of achieving maximum reliability of data.

Once data is gathered, it needs to be interpreted. Very little is said in the literature about the interpretation of data from needs analysis. Researchers seem to assume that the materials evaluator has the skills of analyzing and interpreting data. From my experience, data collection and data analysis or interpretation are two completely different things. The value of any data lies in the way it is interpreted. Therefore, data interpretation is the most critical stages as needs analysts make sense of the data they have gathered and use that data to take decisions about learning and teaching. I shall try to give the reader some tips that will hopefully be useful in tackling this complex part of needs analysis. The type of information that needs analysis can yield will depend on the nature and extent of the procedure undertaken. Some needs analysis exercises are more extensive and tap on more information sources than others and therefore result in more extensive data. Below are examples of the information that needs analysis can produce.

- Who the learners are
- The learners' current level of the language
- Their interests
- Their learning preferences
- Their attitudes
- Their goals and expectations
- Target contexts when the target language is used

When data is gathered in its raw format, it is likely to be in a mass. The data might be qualitative or quantitative. The data analyst's role will be to give meaning to the information gathered. Analyzing data means determining how to organize, synthesize and interrelate the different issues present in it. Since data can be analyzed and interpreted in many different ways, it is advisable to involve other people in the process. This would help avoid subjectivity in the interpretation and will result in greater understanding of the data. In some cases, the data will need to be compared with other criteria, standards or benchmarks. For example, if learners are given a test as a way to measure their language proficiency, their performance should ideally be measured against standardized language proficiency levels. The following task will demonstrate the different instruments that are popular in needs analysis.

Task

Look at the list of situations below and decide about the best instrument(s) you would use for needs analysis based on the nature of the course. You need to hypothesize about the different aspects of the course, such as level of the students, their workplace, etc. Once you have decided about the best instrument for each situation, compare your work with other students. Discuss your choices.

In order to help you decide about the best instrument for your course/situation, it would be good to think of a context, an imaginary context, where the course would be taught. Once you have defined your context, choose one or two instruments that you would use to collect information about the learners' needs. Then write a brief description for each instrument.

Table 2.2. Needs analysis instruments and audience in different situations

No.	Situation	Instrument	Target audience
1	An English course for taxi drivers		
2	An English course for mechanics		
3	An English course for office secretaries		
4	An English course for hospital housekeepers		
5	An English course for children (3–5 years old)		
6	An English course for pilots		
7	An English course for housemaids		

Now look at the third column in Table 2.2. Think about the people you would need to elicit information from about each situation. Again, compare notes with another student and discuss your choices.

The outcome from needs analysis is a list of the literacy requirements that learners need in their use of the target language. This should include the competencies that enable learners to perform the tasks. One important point to consider at this stage is that the materials evaluator's beliefs about language learning and teaching will inevitably affect their interpretation of the data.

However, one way to reduce the effect of beliefs is to get other perspectives on the analysis and the interpretation.

Once needs are determined, decisions about the most suitable materials should be made. It would be difficult to find a single commercial textbook that caters for the precise needs of a particular group of learners. It is therefore advisable that more than one textbook be selected and piloted before any of them is finally adopted for use. Many commercial textbooks claim that they have been designed 'with learners' needs in mind'. Like any business, publishing is also concerned with maximizing profit. As a result, textbooks are sometimes seen as a 'commodity' that must sell. To achieve this, publishers try all means to market their materials. They 'cast their net' quite widely in order to capture as many users as possible. This invariably comes at a cost as it would be quite impossible to write materials to respond to specific needs while at the same time target a very wide audience.

When reviewing materials, evaluators should consider the pedagogical aspects of the materials, in terms of presentation, methodology, etc. Information about such aspects may not be easily evident in the needs analysis data or in the materials themselves. The appropriateness of the methodology adopted by a certain textbook to the learning situation also depends on the teachers' preferences and beliefs which should be sought in the needs analysis stage. In fact, for more successful and effective learning and teaching, teachers should be involved throughout the stages of the review. "If teachers are not enthused by materials their dissatisfaction is always apparent to the learners, the materials lose credibility and the learners motivation and investment of energy are reduced" (Tomlinson, 1998, pp. 146–147).

However, materials evaluators and teachers should first identify the learners' needs and then match them with the closest materials. Material adaption is inevitable in the field of English language teachers. Teachers almost always find themselves having to supplement the materials assigned to the course. Many teachers actually welcome that and see this as an opportunity to use their creativity and connect the course more closely to the learners' needs.

It is hoped such an extensive needs analysis will yield important data that materials evaluators could then confidently use as criteria for vetting any teaching material.

CONCLUSION

Needs analysis is the forgotten basis for the materials evaluation. Materials evaluators often rely on readymade checklists that have been generically designed for a wide range of materials. Such checklists do not normally take into account the specific needs of the learners. Also, in such situations, learners do not normally have the chance to express their views about the new materials. Needs analysis gives learners the opportunity to be part of the decision making process rather than wait until the material has been adopted and used. However, materials evaluators should remember that needs are not normally clear and straightforward. Identifying needs requires the selection of suitable instruments, identification of the right informants and the right analysis and interpretation of the data. Once needs are established, it will be much easier for the materials evaluator to select the teaching materials that best fit the learners' needs. There are certain guidelines that the materials evaluators can consult in carrying their needs analysis.

REFERENCES

Cunningsworth, A. (1995). *Choosing your coursebook*. Oxford: Heinemann.
Daoud, A., & Celce-Murcia, M. (1979). Selecting and evaluating a textbook. In M. Celce-Murcia & L. McIntosh (Eds.), *Teaching English as a second or foreign language* (pp. 302–307). Cambridge, MA: Newbury House Publishers.
Hamidi, H., Bagheri, M., Sarinavaee, M., & Seyyedpour, A. (2016). Evaluation of two general English textbooks: New interchange 2 vs. four corners 3. *Journal of Language Teaching and Research, 7*(2), 345–351.
Hutchinson, T., & Waters, A. (1987). *English for specific purposes*. Cambridge: Cambridge University Press.
Mukundan, J., & Nimehchisalem, V. (2012). Evaluative criteria of an English language textbook evaluation checklist. *Journal of Language Teaching & Research, 3*(6), 1128–1134.
Nation, I. S., & Macalister, J. (2009). *Language curriculum design*. New York, NY & London: Routledge.
Reviere, R. (1996). *Needs assessment: A creative and practical guide for social scientists*. Washington, DC: Taylor & Francis.
Roberts, J. (1996). Demystifying materials evaluation. *System, 24*(3), 375–389.
Sheldon, L. E. (1988). Evaluating ELT textbooks and materials. *ELT Journal, 42*(4), 237–246.
Skierso, A. (1991). Textbook selection and evaluation. In M. Celce-Murcia (Ed.), *Teaching English as a second or foreign language* (pp. 432–453). Boston, MA: Heinle and Heinle Publishers.
Tajeddin, Z., & Teimournezhad, S. (2015). Exploring the hidden agenda in the representation of culture in international and localised ELT textbooks. *The Language Learning Journal, 43*(2), 180–193.
Titcomb, A. (2000). *Needs analysis: ICYF evaluation concept sheet*. Tucson, AZ: University of Arizona.
Tomlinson, B. (1998). Comments on part B. In B. Tomlinson (Ed.), *Materials development in language teaching* (pp. 146–148). Cambridge: Cambridge University Press.
Witkin, B. R., & Altschuld, J. W. (1995). *Planning and conducting needs assessments: A practical guide*. Thousand Oaks, CA: Sage Publications.

Saleh Al-Busaidi
College of Education
Sultan Qaboos University
Sultanate of Oman

DARÍO LUIS BANEGAS

3. EVALUATING LANGUAGE AND CONTENT IN COURSEBOOKS

INTRODUCTION

English language teaching coursebooks, as cultural artifacts in formal education (Gray, 2010; on cultural representations see Tajeddind & Teimournezhadb, 2014), are not simply an end-product. They are developed through a complex circuit which includes market analysis, design, piloting, distribution, and Ministry approval in some contexts, implementation and use (McGrath, 2013). Such a circuit is inevitably permeated by contextual forces and affordances which enter in a dialogic relationship with the ELT curriculum, planning, and practice as illustrated in the literature (Atai & Mazlum, 2013; Ghorbani, 2009; Jahangard, 2007; Tahmasebi, Ghaedrahmat, & Haqverdi, 2013; Sabet & Sadeh, 2012).

The role which teachers play in this circuit is paramount. They are in charge of implementing, adopting, and, probably or expectedly, adapting coursebooks. In other words, teachers bring coursebooks to life and not necessarily in ways naively expected by their authors. Teachers are critical and active agents and not robots following a teacher's guide (Kiai, 2013). They need to evaluate coursebooks according to their context, learners' needs, institutional needs, and the approach which they seek to explore.

In this chapter, I focus on evaluating language and content in coursebooks following CLIL (Content and Language Integrated Learning), where the language is English as a foreign language (EFL). I first provide reasons why teachers should evaluate coursebooks whatever their approach. Secondly, I offer a brief outline of CLIL and how it may be found in coursebooks. Thirdly, I suggest ways in which teachers can decide if a coursebook is worth adopting under a CLIL framework.

TEACHERS AS COURSEBOOK EVALUATORS

In a thorough review of materials development in ELT, Tomlinson (2012) addresses key aspects such as evaluation criteria, writers' perspectives, and the value of coursebooks among others. In relation to this last aspect, Tomlinson (2012, p. 158) raises a crucial issue: teachers' empowerment:

> Opponents of coursebooks argue that they can disempower both teacher and learners, cannot cater for the needs and wants of their actual users, are used

mainly to impose control and order (e.g., 'OK, class, turn to page 46 of your coursebook', Mukundan, 2009b, p. 99), and provide only an illusion of system and progress.

When the perception that coursebook disempower teachers is inscribed in our practices, teachers can challenge this view by turning into evaluators of the coursebooks they use or wish to use. McGrath (2013, p. 105) notes that "coursebooks are normally an investment, in more ways than one", and this entails that teachers need to become critical users and consumers of marketed materials in order to match their own aims with those in a coursebook. However, this does not mean regarding a coursebook as a given, an inherent element in our practices, or the only resource we should benefit from. There are other types of materials (see Stanley, 2013) and there could also be lessons with almost no materials (see Thornbury, 2013).

Even when coursebook choice is not in the hands of teachers, they can still evaluate them in order to enrich them with context-responsive teacher-made materials and become authors of their practices, pedagogies and materials. Taking a coursebook as an exercise is another way of professional development individually or collaboratively. However, McGrath (2013) observes that teachers who are not usually in a position to make decisions on coursebooks cannot be asked to evaluate them without any guidance or support from coordinators or department heads. Coursebook evaluation needs to be a systematic activity, and by systematic I mean an activity based on informed and supported views that make room for inter-subjectivity rather than personal feelings or random perceptions.

Teachers should approach coursebook evaluation from a constructive and positive perspective. In other words, they need to see the extent to which a coursebook matches their aims and context and in what ways they can enrich it with other materials. That said, we may agree that there is no perfect coursebook and that we will always find something lacking or missing. In this regards, we need to remind ourselves that a coursebook is not the solution to all our problems, but one tool to help us create our own responses.

CLIL AND COURSEBOOKS

As I mentioned above, teachers can be guided and empowered through coursebook evaluation by providing them with the rationale behind a coursebook and the approach their practices and coursebooks should respond to. Although we believe that the rationale and approach behind a coursebook are the result of connections between theory and practice which usually appear in the teacher's book, Tomlinson (2013) still urges coursebook writers to produce principled materials, that is, ELT materials based on second language acquisition theory and research.

That said, I offer below a brief summary of CLIL before engaging in suggestions based on CLIL-driven coursebooks:

CLIL is an approach which condenses practices through which learners develop foreign language learning together with curriculum content. It is underpinned by sociocultural concepts such as scaffolding and mediation, and contributions from the cognitive front such as higher and lower thinking skills (see Muñoz, 2007).

According to Cenoz (2013), CLIL could be conceptualized and implemented as an educational approach or a language teaching approach. Such a differentiation seems to respond to the fact that CLIL could be adopted through two macro models: content-driven (CLIL as an educational approach, see also Dalton-Puffer & Nikula, 2014) or language-driven (CLIL as a language teaching approach). On the other hand, it also seems to respond to what I call the *geographies of CLIL*, i.e. the sociocultural settings where it is implemented and the resources available. CLIL in Europe is becoming content-driven, but in other places, CLIL is seen as an opportunity to revitalise the ELT curriculum only. In line with this last view, Hall (2011, p. 195) wonders: "what is the relationship between CLIL and 'strong' forms of CLT?" In the paragraphs below, I discuss both content- and language-driven CLIL in more detail.

Content-driven CLIL refers to the teaching of a subject, for example History or Science, through a language other than the usual language of instruction, for example English in Spain (see Morton, 2013). In this model, the focus is on learning the subject matter or curriculum content and another language at the same time. In this model, learners learn for example, Science, and the specific genre, grammar, and lexis, to talk about different Science contents (see Llinares, Morton, & Whittaker, 2012). Activities and resources scaffold both content and language learning (see Chadwick, 2012; Deller & Price, 2007). Assessment is holistic but may favour content over language as, in most cases, subject-matter or non-language teachers proficient in the target language, are in charge of the lessons. Those familiar with bilingual education (see Abello-Contesse et al., 2013) or immersion programs (see Somers & Surmont, 2012) may see that CLIL is not truly innovative or original.

On the other hand, language-driven CLIL refers to the incorporation of curricular content into the EFL lessons. These lessons remain in the ELT teachers' hands and they may seek support from their non-language colleagues. While the aim is to learn content and language together, activities, materials, and assessment prioritize language over content. In relation to the curricular content, this needs to be new to the learners or familiar to them to some extent. For example, learners may know about poetry and stylistics in their L1 and through CLIL they may learn about poetry and literary movements in the UK.

In relation to content, two clarifications are needed. First, the content should be curriculum-related. If the lessons integrate language with any content, then it may be seen as a topic-based lesson, something usually found in task-based learning or communicative language teaching. Secondly, the curricular content needs to provide a cognitive challenge and be original. This clarification is necessary because some teachers and administrators may wrongfully believe that CLIL means teaching the same content twice, that is, through two different languages (e.g. Persian and English). CLIL becomes a motivating approach when the contents are a novelty, there is an element of authenticity of purpose (Pinner, 2013), and learners' voices are sought to encourage involvement, discovery and awareness (Banegas, 2013; Coyle, 2013).

Language also deserves some clarifications. Language learning should be presented through all skills (speaking, listening, reading, and writing). Furthermore, language teaching in CLIL should help learners not only expand their content-specific vocabulary but also the language needed to talk about the content and solve the different tasks proposed by the teacher. These recommendations have been skillfully integrated into the language triptych (Coyle, Hood, & Marsh, 2010). The triptych includes: (1) language of learning, i.e. content-specific terminology, (2) language for learning, i.e. language to, for example, compare two rivers or two historical events (comparative adjectives, linkers, etc.) and (3) language through learning, i.e. language needs which emerge from the teaching and learning processes.

Overall, CLIL is based on learning curricular content and another language with others and scaffolded through materials which offer opportunities for language and cognitive development. In the section which follows, I discuss the extent to which these features are found in the language-driven CLIL market.

CLIL IN COURSEBOOKS

There is growing interest in producing guidelines for developing CLIL materials aimed at authors and teachers (see Evans, James Hartshorn, & Anderson, 2010; Mehisto, 2012; Meyer, 2010). In general, such guidelines stress the aspects which I list below:

- Cohesion
- Stability
- Flexibility
- Responsiveness connected to the curriculum
- Contextualized sources of input and activities
- Cognitive-rich and language-rich texts
- Inclusion of authentic sources and tasks

However, there are only a few publications which examine CLIL materials. In Argentina, where CLIL can be found as language-driven in state schools but also as content-driven in private bilingual schools, Banegas (2014) investigated how CLIL is represented in general English coursebooks. To this effect he analyzed four series adopted by teachers in Argentina and found:

(1) little correlation between featured subject specific content and school curricula in L1, (2) oversimplification of contents and (3) dominance of reading skills development and lower-order thinking tasks. (Banegas, 2014, p. 345)

Towards the content end of CLIL, Morton (2013) investigated teachers' use of CLIL materials in four European countries (Austria, Finland, Spain, and the

Netherlands). Through an online survey and data from a multi-case study, the author found that:

- Teachers did not tend to use materials designed for native speakers.
- Teachers adapted authentic materials in line with their teaching aims.
- Teachers developed their own materials from scratch.
- Teachers were mostly concerned with appropriateness of materials for learners in terms of content, language, and context.

Both Banegas (2014) and Morton (2013) suggest that the market cannot cater for all teachers' needs and contexts, and that teachers may create their own materials. Nonetheless, they suggest that coursebooks are still a useful organizing tool for teachers.

Unfortunately, this section cannot go any further for an interest in published CLIL materials is incipient. While we can find CLIL books mainly produced for the European market particularly aimed at secondary education schools which adopt CLIL as an educational approach, the CLIL-coursebook market for ELT, CLIL as a language learning approach, is still at an embryonic stage. At the same time, I do not wish to address the possibility of teachers as CLIL material developers. That deserves a self-contained publication elsewhere. However, teachers can refer to different publications (Mehisto, 2012; Meyer, 2010; Mehisto, Marsh, & Frigols, 2008).

EVALUATING CLIL IN COURSEBOOKS: WHAT TO LOOK FOR

English language teachers wishing to explore CLIL through marketed coursebooks can choose:

a. Coursebooks written in English as the L1 for students in English-speaking countries.
b. General English language learning coursebooks internationally commercialised.
c. Specially written CLIL coursebooks, which have a European audience in mind.

I am confident that teachers can find and create other alternatives, but below I discuss the options above. Through questions, I provide suggestions on what to look for based on my experience as a teacher. I must clarify that the bullet-point questions which follow are merely a guide of what teachers may look for. I hope that my own informed decisions and explorations serve as the basis for coursebook evaluation in terms of language and content.

Coursebook Written in English as the L1

In my identity as a teacher I usually enrich my lessons with coursebooks targeted at learners in mainstream education in the UK. For example, I use A-level study guides for Geography, History, and Literature to expand on a reading text in an ELT coursebook.

Above all, I consider my learners' motivations, needs, and development and the curriculum which I am expected to respond to. With these factors in mind, I take a Geography study guide for example and I ask myself:

- Does the coursebook contain contents and ideologies which are similar to my own curriculum? If it doesn't, how can I make links or provide learners with different views?
- To what extent is it UK-driven? Are there 'international' topics?
- Is it easy to purchase and affordable? Are there any restrictions?
- Is the language accessible?
- Is the book content-rich and language-rich?
- Does it encourage lower- as well as higher-order thinking skills?
- Are texts broken down into manageable units? If not, how can I achieve that?
- Does it contain summaries?
- Does it contain graphics and useful visual support to scaffold learning?
- Does it include a companion website with free access activities?
- Does it come with activities, boxes with key words, or a glossary? If it doesn't, how can I create activities based on the texts offered?
- If there are activities, does it include answer keys for self-study or peer correction and reflection?
- Does it offer flexibility in terms of content organization? Can I start with Unit 3 and then cover Unit 1?

Even if I choose one among several options, I know that I do not need to follow it strictly as if it were a script. More importantly, I need to ensure that even learners with a low level of English, whatever this means, can still profit from more complex texts. I always have in mind Tomlinson's (2008) position of approaching materials as language learning materials and that we should not treat linguistically low level learners as intellectually low level learners.

General English Language Learning Coursebooks

I must admit that I am more critical with ELT coursebooks for a number of reasons: (1) I am a teacher of English, (2) coursebooks writers are ELT experts or knowledgeable of our field, and (3) coursebooks still dominate the ELT scene. When I wish to adopt a general English coursebook with a CLIL component, I ask myself the following questions:
- What target audience does the book aim at?
- Is CLIL included as a regular or add-on component?
- Is a given curricular content the core of a unit? Does it appear as decorative/ illustrative or disjointed from the rest of the unit?
- Is the content relevant and cognitively challenging, yet, scaffolded?
- Is the content related to my school curriculum or is it just 'any content or topic'?
- Is content presented through different oral, audiovisual, and written formats?

- If it is presented only through reading, do the activities promote higher-order thinking skills and content appropriation? Or are they simply superficial reading comprehension questions?
- Is the language accessible and scaffolded?
- Is the language found in the content section part of the unit in which it is included? Is there evidence of recycling and sequencing?
- Are there activities which integrate content and language through activities which focus on vocabulary, syntax, and (subject-specific) discourse?
- Are there activities to promote language of/for/through learning?
- Do activities and texts integrate a focus on forms as well as meaning?

As teachers we need to look for general English coursebooks where CLIL is systematic and responsibly included rather than CLIL as a watered down alternative. In addition, the content needs to be cognitively stimulating and differ from contents usually found in ELT coursebooks (see Banegas, 2014). Otherwise we may run the risk of naming CLIL something that may as well be named topic-based learning or simply communicative learning.

CLIL Coursebooks

Although CLIL coursebooks are relatively new and tend to be European-focused, teachers may wish to consider this option because the coursebook approach and rationale are (or should be) based on CLIL research and theoretical underpinnings.

We may agree that the questions I posited for general English coursebooks with a CLIL component may also be applicable for CLIL coursebooks. However, I should remark that the activities must take learners from lower to higher-order thinking skills and that the content should be complex enough in order to ensure cognitive development and motivation. Furthermore, the coursebook should aim at providing learners with language of/for/through learning and features of subject-specific discourse through awareness raising and explicit notes.

I include below some guiding questions to help teachers decide whether they wish to adopt a CLIL coursebook:

- Do the coursebook contents reflect my curriculum and learners' interests as well as needs?
- Is there variety in terms of sources of input and activities?
- Is the language too easy or too difficult?
- Are there authentic texts or modified texts?
- Is the content too easy or too difficult?
- Are contents related and sequenced?
- Is the coursebook internally coherent and cohesive?
- Is it flexible? Can I skip parts? Can I change the order in which units are presented?

CONCLUSION

Whatever the choices and informed decisions made by teachers, it is essential that learners and their context are assessed against coursebooks and our CLIL aspirations. By context I do not only mean the geographical and institutional location but also the curriculum, educational policies, educational practices, and teachers' views. The coursebook needs to be taken as a tool, not a corset. It should open windows rather than restrict practices.

We may agree that evaluating a coursebook is not an easy task because our decision will have an impact on our teaching and learning practices. Nonetheless, coursebook evaluation is also an ongoing process that we carry as we use a coursebook. Along these lines, coursebook evaluation is a process that starts before we teach a course and continues even after we finish with the course.

Last, evaluating coursebooks within a CLIL approach should be seen as a professional development opportunity to be carried out collaboratively. Teachers need to ensure that content and language are treated holistically but with instances to practice both separately and together through different activities.

REFERENCES

Abello-Contesse, C., Chandler, P. M., López-Jiménez, M. D., & Chacón-Beltrán, R. (Eds.). (2013). *Bilingual and multilingual education in the 21st century: Building on experience.* Bristol: Multilingual Matters.

Atai, M. R., & Mazlum, F. (2013). English language teaching curriculum in Iran: Planning and practice. *Curriculum Journal, 24*(3), 389–411.

Banegas, D. L. (2013). The integration of content and language as a driving force in the EFL lesson. In E. Ushioda (Ed.), *International perspectives on motivation: Language learning and professional challenges* (pp. 82–97). Basingstoke: Palgrave Macmillan.

Banegas, D. L. (2014). An investigation into CLIL-related sections of EFL coursebooks: Issues of CLIL inclusion in the publishing market. *International Journal of Bilingual Education and Bilingualism, 17*(3), 345–359.

Cenoz, J. (2013). Discussion: Towards an educational perspective in CLIL language policy and pedagogical practice. *International Journal of Bilingual Education and Bilingualism, 16*(3), 389–394.

Chadwick, T. (2012). *Language awareness in teaching: A toolkit for content and language teachers.* Cambridge: Cambridge University Press.

Coyle, D. (2013). Listening to learners: An investigation into 'successful learning' across CLIL contexts. *International Journal of Bilingual Education and Bilingualism, 16*(3), 244–266.

Coyle, D., Hood, P., & Marsh, D. (2010). *Content and language integrated learning.* Cambridge: Cambridge University Press.

Dalton-Puffer, C., & Nikula, T. (2014). Content and language integrated learning. *Language Learning Journal, 42*(2), 117–122.

Deller, S., & Price, C. (2007). *Teaching other subjects through English.* Oxford: Oxford University Press.

Evans, N. W., James Hartshorn, K., & Anderson, N. J. (2010). A principled approach to content-based materials development for reading. In N. Harwood (Ed.), *English language teaching materials: Theory and practice* (pp. 131–156). Cambridge: Cambridge University Press.

Ghorbani, M. R. (2009). ELT in Iranian high schools in Iran, Malaysia and Japan: Reflections on how tests influence use of prescribed coursebooks. *Reflections on English Language Teaching, 8*(2), 131–139.

Gray, J. (2010). The branding of English and the culture of the new capitalism: Representations of the world of work in the English language coursebooks. *Applied Linguistics, 31*(5), 714–733.

Hall, G. (2011). *Exploring English language teaching*. Abingdon: Routledge.
Jahangard, A. (2007). Evaluation of EFL materials taught at Iranian public high schools. *Asian EFL Journal, 9*(2), 130–150.
Kiai, A. W. (2013). Am I a robot? English language teachers on teachers' guides. *Argentinian Journal of Applied Linguistics, 2*(1), 23–46.
Llinares, A., Morton, T., & Whittaker, R. (2012). *The roles of language in CLIL*. Cambridge: Cambridge University Press.
McGrath, I. (2013). *Teaching materials and the roles of EFL/ESL teachers: Theory and practice*. London & New York, NY: Bloomsbury.
Mehisto, P. (2012). Criteria for producing CLIL learning material. *Encuentro, 21*, 15–33.
Mehisto, P., Marsh, D., & Frigols, M. J. (2008). *Uncovering CLIL: Content and language integrated learning in bilingual and multilingual education*. Oxford: Macmillan.
Meyer, O. (2010). Towards quality-CLIL: Successful planning and teaching strategies. *Pulso, 33*, 11–29.
Morton, T. (2013). Critically evaluating materials for CLIL: Practitioners' practices and perspectives. In J. Gray (Ed.), *Critical perspectives on language teaching materials* (pp. 111–136). Basingstoke: Palgrave Macmillan.
Muñoz, C. (2007). CLIL: Some thought on its psycholinguistic principles. *Revista Española de Lingüística Aplicada, 1(Volumen Extraordinario)*, 17–26.
Pinner, R. (2013). Authenticity of purpose: CLIL as a way to bring meaning and motivation into EFL contexts. *Asian EFL Journal, 15*(4), 138–159.
Sabet, M. S., & Sadeh, N. (2012). CLIL European-led projects and their implications for Iranian EFL context. *English Language Teaching, 5*(9), 88–84.
Somers, T., & Surmont, J. (2012). CLIL and immersion: How clear-cut are they? *ELT Journal, 66*(1), 113–116.
Stanley, G. (2013). *Language learning with technology: Ideas for integrating technology in the classroom*. Cambridge: Cambridge University Press.
Tahmasebi, G.-A., Ghaedrahmat, M., & Haqverdi, H. (2013). The relationship between language proficiency and Iranian EFL learners' knowledge of vocabulary depth versus vocabulary breadth. *Latin American Journal of Content and Language Integrated Learning, 6*(2), 96–111.
Tajeddin, Z., & Teimournezhad, S. (2015). Exploring the hidden agenda in the representation of culture in international and localised ELT textbooks. *The Language Learning Journal, 43*(2), 180–193.
Thornbury, S. (2013). Resisting coursebooks. In J. Gray (Ed.), *Critical perspectives on language teaching materials* (pp. 204–223). Basingstoke: Palgrave Macmillan.
Tomlinson, B. (2008). Language acquisition and language learning materials. In B. Tomlinson (Ed.), *English language learning materials: A critical review* (pp. 3–13). London & New York, NY: Continuum.
Tomlinson, B. (2012). Materials development for language learning and teaching. *Language Teaching, 45*(2), 143–179.
Tomlinson, B. (2013). Second language acquisition and materials development. In B. Tomlinson (Ed.), *Applied linguistics and materials development* (pp. 11–31). London & New York, NY: Bloomsbury.

Darío Luis Banegas
University of Warwick
Coventry, UK

THOM KIDDLE

4. EVALUATING TEACHING AIDS

INTRODUCTION

There is a story, possibly apocryphal, of a famous photographer who attended a dinner party thrown by a rich society lady. During the meal, the hostess turned to the photographer, and said in a loud voice, "My dear, you take the most amazing photographs; you must have a fantastic camera". The photographer smiled politely. At the end of the meal the photographer thanked the hostess for inviting him and said in a voice loud enough for the other guests to hear, "I must say, the food was absolutely delicious… you must have a fantastic oven!"

The meaning is clear here, and has a direct parallel for the evaluation of teaching aids in language teaching, and indeed in any educational context. For whatever evaluation we may do of the innate properties and qualities of a particular teaching aid, we must always consider that the true effectiveness will lie in the way the teacher or learners use it in practice, whether that is inside or outside the classroom.

It is important to emphasise this final point, for teaching aids are not only "… the resources and equipment available to us in the classroom, as well as the resources we can bring into the classroom" (Spratt et al., 2005, p. 119), but also the resources which we may introduce learners to for study or practice outside the classroom, and equally those resources learners may introduce teachers to, which help us prepare and conduct our teaching, beyond the physical boundaries of the classroom wall. Within this wider definition, it is hard to definitively draw a line determining what is *not* a potential teaching aid. Should we not consider realia, the immediate environment, and the students and teacher themselves as highly exploitable resources?

Consequently, this chapter will explore approaches to evaluation of physical teaching aids, designed primarily for language teaching and learning, as well as digital tools not explicitly designed for educational purposes but which may have a place in classroom teaching, or in teacher-supported individual or collaborative learning. However, we will not reflect on resources designed for self-study, as these may be considered learning aids, rather than teaching aids.

WHO CONDUCTS THE EVALUATION?

One key question to address from the outset is the question of who is conducting the evaluation, and for what purpose. Approaches to evaluation of teaching aids may include a student-led evaluation, as part of a focus on needs analysis or learning strategies, for example. This could involve learners identifying the resources which will be most useful to them in the processing, storing and practice of lexical phrases, for instance, or a comparison of different online dictionaries.

Conversely, the evaluation may be teacher-led, and related to resources which may be useful and useable for particular course or lesson aims, or learning outcomes, and require a teacher to analyse and evaluate a range of competing options, or to decide whether a single available resource is likely to add to the effectiveness of their teaching. And thirdly, of course, there is the contextual reality in many situations, where, as McGrath (2002, p. 12) notes for textbooks, "... the selection ... may be determined by any one of a number of different individuals or groups other than the teacher who will ultimately use it". This could be a Ministry of Education, as in a decision to equip schools with interactive whiteboards in the UK (see Gillen et al., 2006 for an interesting discussion of this); a state board (US) or equivalent, as in decisions to provide laptops or tablet computers to school children (see the One Laptop per Child initiatives worldwide); or a school principal, department head, director of studies, or similar, deciding on a particular piece of software or the purchase of physical resources such as class sets of graded readers or mini-whiteboards. In all the above situations, the evaluative criteria and procedures will be different in nature and in what influences the considerations and the final outcomes. However, there is no reason why any of them should be excused from an evaluation based on a principled framework.

EVALUATION FRAMEWORKS

Principled frameworks in materials development and resource evaluation come from a need to go beyond "... processes which are ad hoc and spontaneous and which rely on an intuitive feel for activities which are likely to work" (Tomlinson, 2013, p. 95). They should also go beyond criteria which are unexplored and unexplained lists of important-sounding concepts, like 'contemporaneity' (why should this be an issue in the websites we choose when it's rarely an issue in the music we use in the classroom?), 'authenticity' (which was challenged more than 30 years ago by Widdowson's (1979) contrast of authenticity and genuineness) and 'methodology' (can this really be considered a property of a piece of material or resource rather than the teacher's approach to it?).

In a thoughtful and thought-provoking article on the influence of research in second language acquisition on the implementation of educational technology in language teaching, Thornbury (2014) takes up Tomlinson's (2011) challenge and posits a list of key findings in SLA which may be applied to the creation of critical and principled evaluation frameworks. These SLA insights are worth highlighting here for exemplification of the way they have been applied to an analysis of educational technology, and the lessons which may be learned for the broader evaluation of teaching aids. Thornbury's 10 'observations' are:

1. The acquisition of an L2 grammar follows a 'natural order' that is roughly the same for all learners, independent of age, L1, instructional approach, etc., although there is considerable variability in terms of the rate of acquisition and of ultimate achievement (Ellis, 2008), and, moreover, 'a good deal of SLA happens incidentally' (VanPatten & Williams, 2007).
2. The learner's task is enormous because language is enormously complex (Lightbown, 2000).
3. Exposure to input is necessary (VanPatten & Williams, 2007).
4. Language learners can benefit from noticing salient features of the input (Tomlinson, 2011).
5. Learners benefit when their linguistic resources are stretched to meet their communicative needs (Swain, 1995).
6. There is clear evidence that corrective feedback contributes to learning (Ellis, 2008).
7. Learners can learn from each other during communicative interaction (Swain et al., 2002).
8. Fluency is an effect of having a large store of memorized sequences or chunks (Nattinger & DeCarrico, 1992; Segalowitz, 2010).
9. Learning, particularly of words, is aided when the learner makes strong associations with the new material (Sökmen, 1997).
10. All things being equal, the more time (and the more intensive the time) spent learning and using the language, the better (Muñoz, 2012).

These are then used to determine a set of evaluative criteria which are underpinned by each observation in turn, namely: (1) Adaptivity, (2) Complexity, (3) Input, (4) Focus on Form, (5) Output, (6) Feedback, (7) Interaction, (8) Chunks, (9) Personalization, (10) Investment.

In a similar vein, Kiddle (2013) draws on the work of Twiner et al. (2010) on classroom-based observation of the effectiveness of interactive whiteboards, and Hattie's (2008) meta-analysis of studies in education, to suggest a framework for the evaluation of digital language learning materials and resources which encompasses:

- *Multimodality*, The facility afforded by the "new media" for the easy production and use of a multiplicity of modes of representation – sound, image, writing, moving image, speech – in the message-entities that populate the screen.
- *Orchestration*, The role of the teacher in encouraging pupil participation involves the teacher's 'shaping', or orchestration, of the numerous modes and resources used to support learning of planned objectives and unplanned explorations.
- *Participation*, which can relate to "direct participation" – the physical interaction with the resource or material through touch, typing, mouse movement or gesture; "vicarious participation" – watching, reading, or listening to peers'

engagement with the resource or material; and/or "conceptual and verbal participation" – processing and reacting to or responding to one of the previous two types of participation (Twiner et al., 2010).

- *Feedback*, one of the key variables with a positive impact on student achievement: The art of teaching, and its major successes, relate to "what happens next" – the manner in which the teacher reacts to how the student interprets, accommodates, rejects and/or reinvents the content and skills, how the student relates and applies the content to other tasks, and how the student reacts in light of success and failure apropos the content and methods that the teacher taught (Hattie, 2008, p. 2).

The feedback principle applies to all education, but perhaps is most apposite for digital language learning materials, as it is the area which is most difficult to effectively replicate in instances of a-synchronous communication in which a tutor or peer is involved, or in those instances when feedback must necessarily be pre-programmed for the computer to give.

WHAT THEN, ARE THE IMPLICATIONS OF THIS FOR EVALUATING TEACHING AIDS IN LANGUAGE TEACHING AND LEARNING?

To begin, let us consider a physical teaching aid which has been a feature of language classrooms for over a hundred years: the phonemic chart, based on the International Phonetic Association's phonetic alphabet of 1888, itself influenced by the work of Pitman and Sweet earlier in the 19th century (Kemp, 2006), and popularised for the ELT world by Underhill (1994).

The phonemic chart can be considered a key aid in the teaching of English pronunciation and clearly addresses the SLA principle of a focus on form, number 4 in Thornbury's list. It is available in a wide range of formats, from the original Underhill version, through pictorial representations such as those in the English File series (OUP) to interactive web-based and app versions produced by the British Council and Macmillan. As such it can be considered a flexible and widely available app, suitable for class (in a wall chart form) and individual use.

It is in its application that we find the most interesting content for evaluation of effectiveness, perhaps analysing its potential in one of the seven modes of use suggested by Underhill (1994).

Mode 1: Sounds are introduced and attached to the chart – teacher introduces new sounds, invites learners to practise them, and helps them to shape the sounds – then points to the chart in order to 'attach' the sound to the chart

Mode 2: Teacher uses the chart to prompt learners to speak – teacher silently points to the symbols on the chart (singly for individual sounds/in sequences for syllables/words), and invites a vocal response from the learners

Mode 3: Learners use the chart to point to what teacher has said – teacher says a sound and the learners respond by silently pointing out the sound on the chart

Mode 4: Learners use the chart to prompt the teacher to speak – learner indicates on the chart any sound – teacher says that without adding any comment, leaving time for learners to assimilate

Mode 5: Teacher uses the chart to point to what learners have said – teacher points out on the chart whatever sounds a learner says – immediate feedback – learners can more quickly learn to distinguish English from non-English pronunciation

Mode 6: Learners use the chart to prompt other learners to speak – learner points out on the chart, other learners provide that sound – teacher observes and provides the sound if needed

Mode 7: Learners use the chart to point to what other learners have said – one learner is pointing out sounds/words spoken by other members of a class – teacher intervenes only when mistakes pass unnoticed by the class.

Here we see that the principled evaluation of the effectiveness of a teaching aid depends on the interaction between the innate properties of the resource itself:

- relationship to principles of SLA
- availability and accessibility for teachers and learners
- accuracy of information/content

and the use to which it is put in the classroom (or self-study) context. This latter use is necessarily evaluated by a consideration of:

- the aims of the learning activity,
- the preparedness of teacher and learners to engage with the resource (i.e., the knowledge of the symbols and sounds in this case)
- the potential for adoption and extension by teachers and learners beyond the target activity

The implications of this for evaluation of other physical teaching aids designed primarily for language learning become apparent.

- Firstly, what are our beliefs about how the resource will promote language learning, and how are these underpinned by the research into second language acquisition?
- Secondly, what are the physical properties of the resource and access to it, which may facilitate or hinder its use in the classroom (or other learning environment)?
- Thirdly, what skills or knowledge on the part of the teacher and learner are necessary prerequisites for effective use of the resource?
- Fourthly, to what extent do we consider the language (or other intended focus) contained in the resource to be an accurate representation of language as it is used?

- Finally, what principles of the intended or actual use of the resource contribute to its usefulness for the language learning objective?

Now, let us extend this principle to consider a digital teaching and learning aid: the screen-capture software Jing, which has been the focus of a number of recent studies (see for example, Stannard, 2008) exploring its versatility as a feedback tool for language learners.

The tool is a free, downloadable piece of software available from the company TechSmith (http://www.techsmith.com/jing.html), which allows five minutes' video recording of whatever is on the user's computer screen along with an accompanying audio commentary from the user. The resulting video can be quickly and simply uploaded to a dedicated website, from where it generates a link to be sent or embedded to any internet-connected recipient. The recipient can view the video and listen to the commentary online at any time.

Its uses in language education have centred around teacher-generated videos where the teacher analyses and gives feedback on written work produced by students (e.g. on a Microsoft Word document), simultaneously highlighting words and phrases for praise or correction using the mouse and/or keyboard and explaining the feedback orally. The student receives a reviewed version of their work alongside a video with the verbal comments.

Although the focus of less research, there is also the clear potential within the tool for student-generated videos describing their revisions, or a chosen image, or asking questions about a piece of language they have found online, for example.

For this teaching aid, following the principles of evaluation suggested earlier, we first turn to the beliefs about language learning. There are potential claims for this resource in a number of Thornbury's observations:

1. The ability of the teacher to focus on areas which are within the zone of proximal development of a learner, according to a natural order, and the exposure to incidental language through the commentary.
2. The fact that this tool can be applied to any piece of language (though limited to 5 minutes in length of video).
3. The input provided by the teacher in the commentary.
4. The focus on form chosen by the teacher.
5. The importance of corrective feedback.
6. The personalisation of the feedback to the learner, and focused on their own language.
7. The opportunity for learning to take place outside the confines of the classroom.

Considering accessibility and availability, although the tool itself is free to download, it is not web-based and so must be installed on each computer on which the user wishes to create videos. The fact that a web connection is necessary for both uploading and viewing of the video content also presents a major accessibility issue, and raises the question of whether digital resources increase inclusiveness for those who cannot physically attend classes, or excludes those who are not connected. Classroom use of this resource also depends on internet access, and whole-class presentation depends on the presence of a computer and projector in the classroom.

As with any digital resource, there is a certain level of technological competence and confidence required to make the resource work effectively, though it is felt that with this particular tool the learning curve is short and not overly steep.

Clearly, the accuracy of information presented through this screen-capture software depends on the individual teacher, and consequently we move into the area of the interaction between the tool itself and the use to which it is put. Claims of the increased impact of feedback delivered through this combination of animated, voiced video (e.g., Mayer, 2001) may be countered by the presence of a short-lived novelty value associated with many technological resources (John & Wheeler, 2008).

There is also the issue of the impact on teacher time and workload of a move towards a large scale use of the tool in providing feedback to large numbers of students across classes, and the implicit transferal of tutor feedback from face-to-face to voiced video.

Therefore, although the specifics involved in critical evaluation of the use of this tool when compared to the classroom-based phonemic chart are very different, the fundamental principles of the evaluation are sufficiently similar to allow us to propose this as a model for evaluation of other digital resources, be they websites, applications, hardware such as interactive whiteboards or the material that is provided for them.

Additionally, it is suggested that a parallel approach would serve in the evaluation of print-based teaching aids such as authentic texts, graded readers, handouts, and supplementary materials. To restate, this comprises:

- beliefs about how the resource will promote language learning, and how are these underpinned by the research into second language acquisition
- the physical properties of the resource and access to it, which may facilitate or hinder its use in the classroom (or other learning environment)
- the skills or knowledge on the part of the teacher and learner which are necessary prerequisites for effective use of the resource
- the extent to which we consider the language (or other intended focus) contained in the resource to be an accurate representation of language as it is used
- the methodological principles of the intended or actual use of the resource and how they contribute to its usefulness for the language learning objective

There may, of course, be considerations given greater priority by others in the decision-making process, not least the cost implications, student, teacher and institutional attitudes, and (perceived) constraints imposed by the syllabus. However, a principled framework such as that highlighted above costs nothing, and equips the teacher with an approach to evaluation which arms them against the twin enemies of a rigid adherence to a prescribed text without supplement or adaptation, and the surfeit of options available when one considers the wide range of teaching aids and resources available in the modern age.

A legend among French sailors tells of a sorcerer who had invented a mill to grind anything the sorcerer required. The mill would only stop when he recited a magic formula. One day a sailor heard of this mill and stole it from the sorcerer. When he reached his boat, the sailor commanded the mill to grind some salt for the cod he planned to catch. Soon his ship was full of salt, but the sailor, unaware of the magic formula, could not stop the mill and it went on and on grinding out salt until the ship sank to the bottom of the sea under the weight of the salt. The mill still lies at the bottom of the sea and gives our oceans their salty taste (Rappoport, 1928).

While the principled framework outlined above is no magic formula, it may allow the ELT teacher increased control over the use of aids and resources available and prevent the language classes from being sunk by addition rather than delicately seasoned.

REFERENCES

Ellis, R. (2008). *The study of second language acquisition* (2nd ed). Oxford: Oxford University Press.
Gillen, J., Staarman, J. K., Littleton, K., Mercer, N., & Twiner, A. (Eds.). (2007). A 'learning revolution'? Investigating pedagogic practice around interactive whiteboards in British primary classrooms. *Learning, Media and Technology, 32*(3), 243–256.
Hattie, J. (2008). *Visible learning: A synthesis of over 800 meta-analyses relating to achievement.* New York, NY: Routledge.
John, P., & Wheeler, S. (2008). *The digital classroom: Harnessing the power of technology for learning and teaching.* London: Routledge.
Kemp, A. (2006). Phonetic transcription: History. In K. Brown (Ed.), *The encyclopaedia of language & linguistics* (2nd ed., Vol. 9, pp. 396–410). Amsterdam: Elsevier.
Kiddle, T. (2013). Developing digital language learning materials. In B. Tomlinson (Ed.), *Developing materials for language teaching* (pp. 189–206). London: Bloomsbury.
Lightbown, P. M. (2000). Anniversary article: Classroom SLA research and second language teaching. *Applied linguistics, 21*(4), 431–462.
Mayer, R. (2001). *Multimedia learning.* Cambridge: Cambridge University Press.
McGrath, I. (2002). *Materials evaluation and design for language teaching.* Edinburgh: Edinburgh University Press.
Muñoz, C. (Ed.). (2012). *Intensive exposure experiences in second language learning.* Bristol: Multilingual Matters.
Nattinger, J. R., & DeCarrico, J. S. (1992). *Lexical phrases and language teaching.* Oxford: Oxford University Press.
Rappoport, A. S. (1928). *Superstitions of sailors.* London: Stanley Paul & Co.
Segalowitz, N. (2010). *Cognitive bases of second language fluency.* London: Routledge.
Sökmen, A. J. (1997). Current trends in teaching second language vocabulary. In N. Schmitt & M. McCarthy (Eds.), *Vocabulary: Description, acquisition and pedagogy* (pp. 237–257). Cambridge: Cambridge University Press.
Spratt, M., Pulverness, A., & Williams, M. (2005). *The TKT (Teaching Knowledge Test) course.* Cambridge: Cambridge University Press.
Stannard, R. (2008). Screen capture software for feedback in language education. In M. Thomas (Ed.), *Proceedings of the second international wireless ready symposium interactivity, collaboration and feedback in language learning technologies* (pp. 16–20). NUCB Graduate School.

Swain, M. (1995). Three functions of output in second language learning. In G. Cook & B. Seidlhofer (Eds.), *Principle and practice in applied linguistics: Studies in honour of H. G. Widdowson* (pp. 125–144). Oxford: Oxford University Press.

Swain, M., Brooks, L., & Tocalli-Beller, A. (2002). Peer-peer dialogue as a means of second language learning. *Annual Review of Applied Linguistics, 22*, 171–185.

Thornbury, S. (2014). *How could SLA research inform EdTech?* Retrieved June, 2014, from http://eltjam.com/how-could-sla-research-inform-edtech/

Tomlinson, B. (2011). Introduction: Principles and procedures of materials development. In B. Tomlinson (Ed.), *Materials development in language teaching* (2nd ed., pp. 1–34). Cambridge: Cambridge University Press.

Tomlinson, B. (2013). Developing principled frameworks for materials development. In B. Tomlinson (Ed.), *Developing materials for language teaching* (pp. 107–129). London: Bloomsbury.

Twiner, A., Coffin, C., Littleton, K., & Whitelock, D. (2010). Multimodality, orchestration and participation in the context of classroom use of the interactive whiteboard: A discussion. *Technology, Pedagogy and Education, 19*(2), 211–223.

Underhill, A. (1994). *Sound foundations*. London: Heinemann Educational Books.

VanPatten, B., & Williams, J. (2007). *Theories in second language acquisition: An introduction*. Mahwah, NJ: Lawrence Erlbaum Associates.

Widdowson, H. G. (1979). *Explorations in applied linguistics*. Oxford: Oxford University Press.

Thom Kiddle
Norwich Institute for Language Education
Norwich, UK

CARLOS RICO-TRONCOSO

5. ASSESSING INTERCULTURAL COMMUNICATIVE COMPETENCE

Towards an Intercultural Approach to Language Teaching and Evaluation

INTRODUCTION

For the last two decades, people have been able to mobilize more effortlessly around the world, and nowadays our societies experience intercultural encounters in which people can communicate more easily regardless of the differences in terms of religion, sex, political ideology, cultural background and language, among others. The purpose of this chapter is to reflect upon the importance of the new trends of the communicative approach for language teaching and evaluation, specifically the importance of the Intercultural Approach for language education and the way this competence can be assessed within communicative activities.

Today, societies are multicultural entities where individuals display and share multiple identities. Byram and Fleming (1998) assert that these identities bind them to particular social groups and their cultural practices. It is clear that in multicultural societies language becomes not only the means of reference but also the instrument that carries cultural meanings that help to maintain a speaker's sense of belonging to particular social groups.

The central question of the debate is to what extent communities are prepared to deal with these new ways of intercultural exchanges, and more specifically, how to deal with divergence and diversity in a context where interlocutors portray different social identities. In theory, one way of being able to deal effectively and appropriately with diversity, whether ethnic, racial, religious or cultural, is by means of Intercultural Communicative Competence (ICC).

WHAT IS INTERCULTURAL COMMUNICATIVE COMPETENCE (ICC)?

ICC has been defined in multiple ways, Fantini has defined ICC as the "ability to deal with differences in a positive manner" (2000, p. 25), and it entails "an individual's ability to communicate and interact across cultural boundaries" (Byram, 1997, p. 7). This chapter will understand ICC not as an ability, but as the overall social and psychological capacity of an individual to manage encounters with people from other cultural backgrounds appropriately (Bennett, 2004; Byram et al., 2001;

Corbett, 2003; Deardorff, 2008; Holliday et al., 2004; Ildikó et al., 2007; Savicki, 2008; Sercu et al., 2005).

When people interact in a foreign language, neither the shared meanings nor the shared values conveyed through language can be taken for granted. Byram and Fleming state that "learning a language as it is spoken by a particular group is learning the shared meanings, values and practices of that group as they are embodied in the language" (1998, p. 2). To understand the shared meanings, individuals have to decentre the self and take up the role of the other. In doing so, they need to develop some capacities associated with the dimensions of ICC which Byram (1997) has listed as in Figure 5.1.

Figure 5.1. Dimensions and components of ICC

- *Savoir* (knowledge) refers to knowledge of self and other; of how interaction occurs; of the relationship of the individual to society.
- *Savoir-faire/savoir comprendre* (skills) deals with knowing how to interpret and relate information.
- *Savoir-s'engager* (awareness) is concerned with knowing how to engage with the political consequences; being critically aware of cultural behaviours.
- *Savoir-faire/savoir apprendre* (skills) refers to knowing how to discover cultural information.
- *Savoir-être* (attitudes-traits) deals with knowing how to be: how to relativise oneself and value the attitudes and beliefs of the other.

To understand clearly what ICC means, it is necessary to think of a communicative situation in which people – from different cultures or backgrounds – interact and bring to the situation their knowledge, their awareness of similarities and differences, their beliefs, their attitudes, their behaviours, their skills and their language(s) to negotiate meanings and establish effective interpersonal relationships. It is clear that in this process none of the interlocutors are *tabula rasas*. They bring to the situations all their experiences and knowledge (*savoirs*) and negotiate them in interactions.

In this process the intercultural speakers have to show their abilities to "interact with *others*, to accept others perspectives and perceptions of the world, to mediate between different perspectives, to be conscious of their evaluations of difference" (Byram et al., 2001, p. 5). In the same vein, Byram (1997) claims that a "successful communication might not be viewed as efficiency of information exchange" (p. 3). On the contrary, we should value the ability of the individuals to establish and maintain relationships.

Traditionally, Foreign Language Teaching (FLT) viewed communication as the process of exchange of information or sending and receiving messages. In that sense, most language teaching materials produced in the last decades spread such a concept. According to this concept, in the process of communication one knows and possesses the information and the other requests and overlooks part of such information. In my view, this has been one of the weaknesses of the Communicative Approach in language teaching. Communication is not seen as an intercultural encounter where individuals continuously negotiate cultural meanings. Byram (1997) states that "even the exchange of information is dependent upon understanding how what one says or writes will be perceived and interpreted in another cultural context; it depends on the ability to decentre and take up the perspective of the listener or reader" (p. 3).

In FLT, when we hear about the Communicative Approach the first names that emerge among others are: Hymes, Austin, Searle, Canale and Swain, Brumfit, Wilkins and Habermas who stand against "linguistic", "grammatical", "structural", "formal" approaches to language evaluation. The main distinction lies in the fact that the formal or structural theories view language outside a particular context of language use, while the communicative theory presents the second language in a more clearly specified context and situation (Stern, 1983, p. 259).

The Communicative Approach is defined on the basis of its object of study – *communicative competence*. If the structural approach focuses on the idea of studying the language as a system composed by sub-systems – phonology, syntax and semantics – and how they operate; the communicative approach should focus on the idea of using and interpreting the language system appropriately in the process of interaction and in relation to social context. That is why Hymes (1972) called "Communicative Competence" the ability to know "when to speak, when not, and as to what to talk about with whom, when, where, in what manner" (p. 277).

We have to clarify that the above mentioned differences were first identified by Chomsky when he made distinctions between *competence* and *performance*.

Competence consists of the mental representation of linguistic rules which constitute the speaker/hearer's internalized grammar. In contrast, performance consists of the comprehension and production of language. The main point of this difference is that only by means of performance we can confirm the existence of competence, because the rules the learner has internalized are not directly observable. They can only be examined when the learner performs, which means that it is mainly through production that "the utterances that the learner produces are treated as windows through which the internalized rule system can be viewed" (Ellis, 1985, p. 6).

In fact, the biggest difference between Chomsky's idea of *competence* and Hymes', according to Duranti (in Kiesling & Bratt, 2005), is that the former relies on the assumption that knowledge can be studied separately from performance, (meant as the implementation of that knowledge in language use), whereas for Hymes, participation, performance, and intersubjective knowledge are all essential features of knowing a language as a whole.

Undoubtedly, communicative competence implies linguistic competence, but its main focus is the intuitive grasp of social and cultural rules and meanings that are carried out by any utterance (Stern, 1983). In this regard, language teaching has to recognize the social, interpersonal, and cultural dimension of language. Here I want to draw attention to the point of how a second/foreign language learner is able to get such "communicative competence" that even a native speaker is not aware of. Then the challenge for language teaching and evaluation are not entirely "teaching the communicative competence". In my own view, it is also important to help the learner develop a third competence – intercultural communicative competence. This competence is understood as the ability to perceive and cope with the differences and similarities between the learner's own culture and the others' culture, in order to mediate and explain differences. Ultimately, ICC intends "to accept that difference, and see the common humanity beneath it" (Zarate quoted by Kramsch in Byram & Fleming, 1998, p. 8).

For now, I only want to point out that when people interact in a language which is foreign at least to one of the speakers, the shared meanings and values that language carries cannot be taken for granted. Precisely because of the assumption that meanings and values are shared, we are not aware of them only until we face breakdowns of communication and/or interaction. As a result, we find it difficult to discriminate them and to understand their significance. "Only after a process of discovering those meanings and practices can learners negotiate and create new reality with their interlocutors, one which is new to both learners and interlocutors, a shared world of interaction and experience" (Byram & Fleming, 1998, p. 3). It is clear that it is not enough to prepare learners for a language, they must also be prepared for the culture(s) they will be exposed to.

The point of the debate is to identify to what extent the CLT contributes to the development of the communicative competence, and further to the development of ICC. Although CLT proposes activities to introduce learners to language as social action, namely dramatizing language use in role-play and simulations, the experience "is a restricted and limited version of using the language in the foreign culture and society, and the principal focus remains on the language, and on the learners' fluency and accuracy in language use" (Buttjes & Byram, 1991, p. 21).

Thanks to the Communicative Approach in language teaching and evaluation, we realized that language users/learners bring together their general capacities – *the general competences* – and the specific language competences – *the communicative competences* – for the realisation of their communicative intentions (see Figure 5.2).

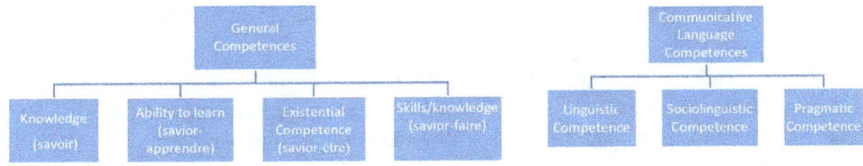

Figure 5.2. Competences for language teaching and learning (CEF, 2001)

To understand what each of these competences refers to, Table 5.1 illustrates the two major competences and what they involve, and it also provides a brief description of each competence. In theory, we see that there are complete taxonomies and proper definitions, but in practice, particularly in our classrooms, there is still a trend to emphasize on aspects that are easy to control and observe – the grammar

Table 5.1. Competences for language teaching, learning and evaluation (adapted from CEF, 2001)

Type of competence	Competencies involved	Main features of the competence
General competence	Knowledge (Savoir)	Declarative knowledge • Knowledge of the world: It is developed through education, experience or it can be derived from information sources. • Socio-cultural knowledge: knowledge of the society and culture, and culture of the community/ies in which a language is spoken. • Intercultural awareness: knowledge, awareness and understanding of the relation (similarities and distinctive differences) between the world of origin and the world of the target community. It includes awareness of regional and social diversity in both worlds. It is also enriched by awareness of a wider range of cultures than those carried by the learner's L1 and L2.

(Continued)

Table 5.1. (Continued)

Type of competence	Competencies involved	Main features of the competence
	Existential competence (Savoir-être)	The communicative activity of users/learners is affected not only by their knowledge, understanding and skills, but also by selfhood factors connected with their individual personalities, characterised by the attitudes, motivations, values, beliefs, cognitive styles and personality types which contribute to their personal identity.
	Ability to learn (savoir apprendre)	Ability to observe and participate in new experiences and to incorporate new knowledge into existing knowledge, modifying the latter where necessary. This ability enables the learner to deal more effectively and independently with new language learning challenges, to see what options exist and to make better use of opportunities. Ability to learn has several components, such as language and communication awareness, general phonetic awareness and skills, study skills and heuristic skills.
	Skills (Savoir-faire)	• Practical skills: social skills, living skills, vocational and professional skills and leisure skills. • Intercultural skills: Relationships within the cultures (origin culture and foreign culture), dealing effectively with misunderstandings within cultures, ability to overcome stereotyped relationships.
Communicative language competence	Linguistic competence	Ability involved in controlling the formal structure of language for producing or recognizing grammatically correct sentences, comprehending their propositional content, and ordering them to form texts (Bachman, 1990). Included in this competence are: grammatical, phonological, semantic, orthographic and orthoepic competence (CEF, 2001).

Table 5.1. (Continued)

Type of competence	Competencies involved	Main features of the competence
	Sociolinguistic competence	Sociolinguistic competence is concerned with the knowledge and skills required to deal with the social dimension of language use. The matters treated here are those specifically relating to language use and not dealt with elsewhere: linguistic markers of social relations; politeness conventions; expressions of folk-wisdom; register differences; and dialect and accent.
	Pragmatic Competence	Pragmatic competences are concerned with the user/learner's knowledge of the principles according to which messages are: a organised, structured and arranged ('discourse competence'); b used to perform communicative functions ('functional competence'); c Sequenced according to interactional and transactional schemata ('design competence').

features. We can conclude, by reference to this table, that it is not enough to master the linguistic code. Today we are required to develop some other competences, including the Intercultural communicative competence (Rico Martín, 2005).

Having introduced the aforementioned competences, the question I want to bring to the discussion is whether we have to "teach" all of them explicitly or whether we have to bring to our classrooms situations for students to deal with them. From my perspective, it is not enough being aware of the existence of those competences. We need to know how to use them in *situated contexts*. In other words, competences are *not taught*, they are *developed*. Following this line of thought, we should expose our students to communicative situations where they have to face the same experiences they tackle in their daily lives when communicating and interacting with *the others*, no matter whether it is in the native language or in the foreign/second language. Up to this point it is necessary to know how to assess and develop ICC when teaching a language.

HOW CAN ICC BE ASSESSED?

Three practical considerations related to ICC learning approach might be taken into account for answering this question: the need to promote an experiential learning, the need to have a structured approach to intercultural learning and the need to link the intercultural learning to language learning. Intercultural learning implies *experiential learning* (Kolb, 1984; Moon, 2004; Tomlinson, 2003). It is not sufficient to read books or to listen to lectures about other cultures. It is necessary to be confronted with new unknown situations, to experience insecurity, fear, rejection as well as security, trust and sympathy, and to deal with the subject of culture on an emotional level. In fact, language teachers can make this possible when working with communicative tasks where learners experience them emotionally. Generally, intercultural learning approach views communicative tasks as social and cultural tools that enable learners to acquire a language.

Communicative tasks also help students experience new knowledge and connect it with their previous experiences. In so doing, communicative tasks make students experience situations and establish links with personal information (see the appendix of a Spanish unit adapted from Verdía et al. (2008), where some readiness and experiential activities are proposed). The approach of learning experientially is related to how our brain works. According to Fennes and Hapgood (1997), "the left hemisphere is concerned with learning that is analytical, rational, intellectual and numerical, whereas the right hemisphere deals with the experiential, the visual, the imaginative, the intuitive, the spatial" (p. 74). Since culture is reflected in both parts of our personality, activities proposed in the language classroom should address both parts of our brain to guarantee an intercultural learning experience.

Fennes and Hapgood (1997), assert that "the concept of experiential learning means moving in circles from experience to reaction, to reflection, to conceptual understanding, to change behaviour. This means that a pedagogic concept for experiential learning activity has to refer to both cognitive and the affective components of the learning process" (p. 74). It is clear that this experience takes place not only in multicultural classrooms where students hold personal encounters with people from other countries or cultures. It also happens in mono-cultural scenarios where students although belonging to the same culture, yet have different backgrounds. We should not forget that misunderstandings happen in every human interaction. What seemed to be self-evident suddenly is not clear. One's own behaviour, which can be perceived as completely normal, can be seen as totally differently when we relate to the other.

Fennes and Hapgood (1997) claim that intercultural education is a synonym for conflict pedagogy. In interactions we have to cope with different value systems, beliefs, attitudes, views of life and of the world. Consequently, it implies conflict. We know that conflicts are part of being human and should not be avoided. We also learn through crisis. Sometimes there are conflicts that cannot be solved easily and we have to learn about them. It is important that we learn to "recognize, to accept and to carry out the conflict in a democratic way. This process is not pleasant. It can be painful and therefore requires an adequate pedagogy" (p. 75).

At last, experiential learning also implies an exercise of consciousness. When we are exposed to a different culture, we start developing our consciousness. We are aware of our own values, beliefs, lifestyles, habits, and norms and therefore culture.

It is clear that this experience is fundamental for being able to perceive cultures without judging them.

In respect of *the structured approach to intercultural learning*, we know that intercultural learning does not happen incidentally or by chance. Meeting people from different cultures does not assure the development of intercultural communicative competence. Fennes and Hapgood (1997) affirm that "pupils will tend to avoid communication if their language skills are not sufficient or if there is no specific need for communicating with the other cultural group" (p. 76). Also meeting people from different backgrounds does not guarantee that pupils change their prejudices or stereotypes.

In this regard, intercultural learning activities should expose pupils to different cultural situations where they have to confront their own cultural behaviours and reflect upon them. Maybe this is one way pupils gain an awareness of how cultural behaviours differ one from another. In so doing, Fennes and Hapgood (1997) suggest an important element of a pedagogic concept for intercultural communication which is the 'triangular didactic' as opposed to a 'dual didactic'. A 'dual didactic' only deals with the 'me' and the 'you' in a relationship. At the beginning this is very stimulating, as we have seen in some CLT activities, where students get to know each other by communicating about each other's personality, but after a while it becomes superficial.

A 'triangular didactic' involves a three-point relationship: you, me and a common theme or project that is pursued jointly. "Working together on a specific project makes cultural differences and cultural conflicts visible. Intercultural learning means how to deal with these differences and conflicts when doing a common task" (Fennes & Hapgood, 1997, p. 76).

We can have a list of tasks or projects but, of course, they change according to the curriculum and the school. It could be something of general concern, like environmental issues, nuclear energy, European integration, etc. Or, it could be related to politics, economy, society or the culture of the countries, such as comparisons of the educational systems, political decision-making processes, lifestyles, etc. It could also be related to specific subjects like history, science, business, etc. The idea of the projects is that pupils will be learning together and learning from each other.

Finally, we have to say that *language learning is an essential element of intercultural learning*. In bicultural or multicultural classroom situations, a major emphasis is put on the minority cultural language group(s) to learn the teaching language, which is normally the language of the majority culture or language group. Fennes and Hapgood (1997) states that "ideally, teaching would be done bilingually" (p. 77). For the minority culture group(s), being able to communicate in the language of the majority culture and thus to participate – at least to some extent – in its social life is not a choice.

Regarding the approach to language learning in bicultural or multicultural classes, Fennes and Hapgood (1997) propose, "the intercultural language trading" (p. 78). This refers to a pupil-centred language learning methodology where two people

Table 5.2. *Criteria to assess ICC within communicative tasks*

Dimensions	Descriptors
Awareness Does the activity promote a reflection on…?	differences across languages
	differences across cultures
	how context affect/alter interactions with others
	how learners view themselves within their own culture
	how learners view themselves within a different culture
	how learners perceive different cultural identities (race, class, gender, age, ability)
	how contexts affect/alter interactions with others
	respecting multiple and different viewpoints
	social issues(weather changes, poverty, food crisis, etc.)
Attitude Does the activity allow learners to…?	interact with members of the host culture
	learn from hosts, their language
	learn from hosts, their culture
	value their own culture
	value the host culture
	express own opinions and views about different subjects
	express their needs
	express their wants
	interact in a variety of ways, some quite different from those to which the learner might be accustomed
	be flexible in communicating with those who are linguistically different
	be flexible in communicating and interacting with those who are culturally different
Skills Does the activity allow learners to…?	demonstrate flexibility when interacting with persons from different cultures
	understand different models of behaviours within cultures
	avoid making judgments about different cultures (food, dress, sexual orientation)
	avoid sending offending messages to different cultures (food, dress, sexual orientation)
	contrast the host culture with their own
	share opinions
	use a variety of effective strategies when interacting with culturally different people
	demonstrate the capacity to interact appropriately in a variety of situations
	cite socio-political factors to shape the learner's own culture
	cite socio-political factors to shape the learner's host culture
	communicate effectively with people from various cultures in a range of social domains, including age, gender, social status, and other factors

Table 5.2. (Continued)

Dimensions	Descriptors
Knowledge Does the activity allow learners to…?	cite a basic definition of culture
	contrast aspects of the host language and culture with their own
	know the essential norms and taboos (greetings, dress, behaviour, etc.) of their own culture.
	know the essential norms and taboos (greetings, dress, behaviour, etc.) of the host culture
	recognize signs of cultural stress
	know some techniques to maximize their learning of the host language
	know some techniques to maximize their learning of the host culture
	describe their own behaviours in various domains (e.g., social interaction, time orientation, relation to the environment, etc.)
	describe their host's behaviours in various domains (e.g., social interaction, time orientation, relation to the environment, etc.)
	articulate the general history and some socio-political factors which have shaped their own culture
	articulate the general history and some socio-political factors which have shaped the host culture
Language proficiency Does the activity contribute to achieve…?	basic survival needs
	minimum courtesy requirements
	some practice of language features (structures and functions)
	ability to communicate on concrete topics
	ability to communicate using non-verbal language
	ability to communicate ideas in different ways

from different cultures, speaking different languages teach each other their language simply by speaking to the other in their own language until communication is established. Here, the process is interactive and the teacher's role is just to structure and monitor the learning process, to suggest themes, to give assignments and consult with the pupils on how they can learn the language from each other.

To see how to assess activities for the development of ICC we should relate the dimensions and components of ICC. Table 5.2 provides some key elements that teachers and materials developers should take into account when evaluating, adapting and/or developing activities for ICC. Whilst highlighting the fact that these criteria do not constitute the only source, it is just a proposal that could be modified or changed depending on sociocultural variables such as context, people involved, and objectives of the curriculum among others. Additionally, I have to clarify that all descriptors do not necessarily have to be included in the activities. Teachers should select the ones they see as more appropriate for their class.

Having seen this table, the question that arises is of how we can include these dimensions and characteristics in developing activities for ICC? There is a likely answer and it is by means of adopting any available methodology within the CLT that suits such principles (Task based learning, TBL, and Text driven approach, TDA as examples).

We have seen throughout these pages how CLT should contribute to the development of students' intercultural communicative competence. Since the strong principle for CLT is that language is acquired through communication, this approach constitutes a valuable tool to develop students' language competences within an intra or inter-cultural context. Fundamentally, within this approach, there are some methodologies that are more suitable for the development of ICC. As an example I can cite two methodologies: *Task Based Learning* (TBL) and *Text Driven Approach* (TDA). These methodologies are planned for students to develop their abilities to think, reflect and communicate. Additionally, by using these methodologies learners can deal with linguistic and cultural issues at the same time. On the one hand, by means of tasks students can learn a language by experiencing how it is used in communication. On the other hand, by means of texts students engage and experience the acquisition of a language.

Now I want to explain in detail these methodologies and justify the one adopted in the example given in this chapter. Breen (quoted by Ellis, 2003, p. 5) has defined a task as "a work plan that is intended to engage the learner in meaning-focused language use". Thus a task requires "the participants to function primarily as language users in the sense that they must employ the same kinds of communicative processes as those involved in real-world activities" (Ellis, 2003, p. 3).

In turn, Nunan (1999) defines a task as "a piece of work undertaken for oneself or for others, freely or for some reward" (p. 24). Thus, examples of tasks include painting a fence, dressing a child, filling out a form, buying a pair of shoes among other things. Nunan (1999) continues by saying that "by a task means the hundred and one things people do in everyday life, at work, at play, and in-between" (p. 24). In task-based learning, learners do not first acquire language as a structural system and then learn how to use this system in communication but rather actually discover the system itself in the process of learning how to communicate.

One feature of tasks is that they result in some clear outcome, other than simply the use of language. The outcome is a tangible product that involves students in comprehending, manipulating and interacting in the target language while all their attention is on meaning rather than form. In this sense, Ellis (2003) identifies some general characteristics of a task.

1. *A task is a work plan*: it constitutes a plan for learner activity. This takes the form of teaching materials or of ad hoc plans for activities that arise in the course of teaching.
2. *A task involves a primary focus on meaning*: a task seeks to engage learners in using language pragmatically rather than displaying language. It seeks to develop L2 proficiency through communicating. Thus, it requires a primary focus on

meaning. The participants choose the linguistic and non-linguistic resources needed to complete the task.
3. *A task involves real-world processes of language use*: The work plan may require learners to engage in a language activity such as that found in the real world, for example, completing a form.
4. *A task can involve any of the four language skills*: the work plan may require students to (a) listen to or read a text and display their understanding, (b) produce an oral or written text, or (c) employ a combination of receptive or productive skills. A task may require dialogic or mono-logic language use. In this respect, tasks are not different from exercises.
5. *A task engages cognitive processes*: the work plan requires learners to employ cognitive processes such as selecting, classifying, ordering, reasoning, and evaluating information in order to carry out the task.
6. *A task has a clearly defined communicative outcome*: the work plan stipulates the non-linguistic outcome of the task, which serves as the goal of the activity for the learners. The stated outcome of the task serves as the means for determining when participants have completed a task.

Now, with regard to the Text Driven Approach, I have to say that this framework was created by Tomlinson (2003) for materials development and evaluation, that it is based mainly on the idea of how people learn a language. It allows teachers "not only to write principled and coherent materials quickly, effectively and consistently but also to articulate and develop their own theories of language learning and language teaching at the same time" (Tomlinson, 2003).

By using texts, students experience and connect their lives with the situations presented in them. Texts constitute, to some extent, a source of students' exposure to language and culture. Texts are, as previously mentioned, cultural representations by which people communicate feelings, thoughts and views of the world. In fact, texts offer students the possibility to interact with the culture(s), the own and target culture.

Now, the biggest dilemma is to decide which methodology is more appropriate for the purpose of developing activities for ICC. Both methodologies can suit such a purpose. However, decisions should be taken considering not only theoretical reasons, but also practical ones. By practical I mean those reasons that are linked to the syllabus, the context and the students. The common point we agree is that as we know, FLT is concerned with communication and

> this has to be understood as more than exchange of information and sending of messages which has dominated CLT in recent years. Even the exchange of information implies to understand what one says or writes is perceived and interpreted differently in another cultural context. In fact, every interactional process is influenced by our ability to decentre and take up the perspective of the listener or reader. (Byram, 1997, p. 3)

Therefore, we should not see a successful communication as efficiency of information exchange. It should be our ability to establish and maintain relationships.

Furthermore, CLT has devoted much effort in trying to model learners on the 'native speaker' competence. Most activities in CLT are intended for students to follow a model of communication that is always orchestrated by native speakers. In this regard, language teaching and evaluation is predicated on the distinction between native speakers and non-native speakers. Non-native speakers are supposed to learn the rules of the native speaker's standard grammar, vocabulary and idioms. In turn the native speaker is supposed to give the norm against which the non-native speaker's performance is measured. Basically, language teaching has traditionally supported the idea of the native speakers as 'the unique model'.

Byram and Fleming (1998), mention that for CLT, "native speakership brings to its speakers a certain authority associated with authenticity and legitimacy of language use" (p. 16). Consequently, they bring the idea of genuine language and represent credibility and respectability. In this respect Kramsch (quoted in Byram & Fleming, 1998) argues that the native speakers' traditional privilege of being the model for learners, ascribed by teachers and readily accepted by learners themselves, has to be re-evaluated and in fact withdrawn. What she proposes is an *intercultural speaker*, a speaker who is able to establish relationships between his own and other culture, who is able to mediate and explain difference, and who shows empathy with *the other*. Therefore, it is important to explore what an intercultural speaker is and what it means to language teaching.

THE INTERCULTURAL SPEAKER AND LANGUAGE EVALUATION

We have mentioned, more or less, that we cannot continue to think that the best language learner is the one who comes nearest to the native speaker mastery of the grammar and vocabulary of the language, and the one who can therefore 'pass for', or be identified as a 'native', communicating as fluent as natives. This conception must be re-evaluated because people experience different sorts of contacts with languages, even in contexts which are entirely characterised as 'monolingual'. There are many ways in which people get to know each other. As an example, it is amazing to see how children nowadays can interact with people from other cultures without being proficient in the other's language (think about how children chat on the Internet and the way they interact in interactive video games).

It is true that the current scenarios where people interact are varied and diverse. People have to face 'worlds' that are culturally different from their own, and sometimes these differences provoke breakdowns in communication. The question to debate is whether language teachers can help students deal with these breakdowns more appropriately. It is clear that the objective of language teaching and evaluation should not only be defined in terms of the acquisition of communicative competence in a foreign language. Teachers are now required to help learners develop intercultural communicative competence and to evaluate them in this regard.

Being able to deal with intercultural experiences requires that the person possesses a number of intercultural competencies and characteristics. According to Sercu et al. (2005) "these characteristics and competencies have been identified as the willingness to engage in the foreign culture, self-awareness, and the ability to look upon oneself from the outside, the ability to see the world through the others' eyes, the ability to cope with uncertainty, the ability to act as cultural mediator, the ability to evaluate others' points of view, the ability to consciously use culture learning skills and to read the cultural context, and the understanding that individuals cannot be reduced to their collective identities" (p. 2). In this regard, in the context of foreign language teaching, intercultural competence should be linked to communicative competence.

CONCLUSION

To sum up, ICC should be defined as the ability to act appropriately in communicative situations where we display not only our linguistic, sociolinguistic and pragmatic knowledge, but also the knowledge about the other's culture. Intercultural communicative competence and its evaluation, then, builds on communicative competence and enlarges as it incorporates intercultural competence. ICC is characterised by five *savoirs,* as mentioned before, which are integrated and intertwined with some components of communicative competence (knowledge, skills and attitudes). The *savoirs* are as follows (Sercu et al., 2005, p. 4):

- The first *savoir, savoirs* with the plural 's', constitutes the knowledge dimension of the conceptual framework. It has been defined as "knowledge about social groups and their cultures in one's own country, and similar knowledge of the interlocutor's country on the one hand, and similar knowledge of the processes and interaction at individual and societal levels, on the other hand" (Byram, quoted by Sercu et al., 2005, p. 4). These *savoirs* represent the frame of reference of the people living (in) a particular culture. The words and gestures that people use, their behaviours, their values, their symbols, etc. are always culture-bound and carry meaning within a particular community. Apart from culture specific knowledge, people also need to acquire a certain amount of culture-general knowledge that allows them to deal with a large diversity of foreign cultures.
- The second *savoir* has to do with the *savoir-apprendre* and *savoir-comprendre.* These constitute the skills necessary to interact with the others. *Savoir-apprendre* refers to "the capacity to learn cultures and assign meaning to cultural phenomena in an independent way" (Byram & Zarate, cited by Sercu et al., 2005, p. 4). *Savoir-comprendre*, refers to the capacity to interpret and relate cultures. These skills plus knowledge and attitudes are key points to the lifelong learning.
- The third savoir is *savoir-faire*, which refers to the overall ability to act in an interculturally competent way in intercultural contact situations, to take into account the specific cultural identity of one's interlocutor and to act in a respectful and co-operative way (Sercu et al., 2005).

- The fourth savoir is *savoir-être* that refers to the capacity and willingness to abandon ethnocentric attitudes and perceptions and the ability to establish and maintain a relationship between one's own and the foreign culture.
- The fifth savoir is *savoir-s'engager* which is characterised by a critical engagement with the foreign culture under consideration and one's own. Here is put in practice the ability to evaluate critically the one's own and the foreign culture.

What these *savoirs* suggest is that we need to become more aware of our own culture and those of others in order to build a bridge of mutual intercultural understandings. In this regards what teachers and students need, according to Byram and Fleming (1998), is to "develop an attitude of being willing to learn, understand and appreciate the other's culture without loss of their own status, role or cultural identity" (p. 116).

One of the contributions that foreign language teaching and evaluation could make to the development of the former *savoirs* is to help learners understand 'otherness'. In our classrooms students are confronted with the language of other people, their culture, their way of thinking and dealing with the world. Byram (1989) mentions that today there are many situations where people born in the same country are nonetheless perceived to be ethnically foreign. Thus, 'otherness' is a feature of any society which contains more than one ethnic group and, usually as a consequence, more than one natively spoken language (p. 25).

On the other hand, we have to bear in mind that *otherness* in people who are by definition 'foreign' to us is not a threat to our identity. It is indeed a means of maintaining our identity. The concern here is of how to deal with *the other* without causing harm or losing our identity. This reality is evidenced in our multicultural classrooms (and in society in general) where we have to face constant breakdowns in communication. Most of the breakdowns, according to Rico-Troncoso (2010) are due to lack of cultural knowledge (target culture and native culture) lack of proficiency to communicate messages, negative social attitudes manifested in prejudices and stereotypes, lack of awareness of social and cultural differences, and lack of skills to interpret and communicate messages.

The aforementioned causes of breakdowns of communication are evidenced in everyday use of language when we communicate with the others in multicultural scenarios. Sometimes we are aware of them, sometimes we are not. In fact, we have to cope with them appropriately so as 'not to lose the face' when communicating (expression used by Geertz, 1975, in rituals of interaction). Therefore, our role as language teachers goes beyond developing our students' language competences.

REFERENCES

Bachman, L. (1990). *Fundamental considerations in language testing.* Oxford: Oxford University Press.
Bennett, J. M. (2004). Becoming interculturally competent. In J. Wurzel (Ed.), *Towar multiculturalism: A reader in multicultural education* (pp. 62–67). Newton, MA: Intercultural Resource Corporation.
Buttjes, D., & Byram, M. (1991). *Mediating languages and cultures.* Clevedon: Multilingual Matters.
Byram, M. (1989). *Cultural studies in foreign language education.* Clevedon: Multilingual Matters.

Byram, M. (1997). *Teaching and assessing intercultural communicative competence.* Clevedon: Multilingual Matters.
Byram, M., & Fleming, M. (1998). *Language learning in intercultural perspective: Approaches through drama and ethnography.* Cambridge: Cambridge University Press.
Byram, M., Nichols, A., & Stevens, D. (2001). *Developing intercultural competence in practice.* Clevedon: Multilingual Matters.
CEF. (2001). *Common European framework of reference for languages: Learning, teaching, assessment.* Cambridge: Cambridge University Press.
Corbett, J. (2003). *An intercultural approach to English language teaching.* Clevedon: Multilingual Matters.
Deardorff, D. K. (2008). Intercultural competence: A definition, model, and implications for education abroad. In V. Savicki (Ed.), *Developing intercultural competence and transformation: Theory, research, and application in international education* (pp. 32–53). Sterling, VA: Stylus Publishing, LLC.
Duranti, A. (2005). Ethnography of speaking: Toward a linguistics of the praxis. In S. Kiesling & C. Bratt (Eds.), *Intercultural discourse and communication: The essential readings* (pp. 17–32). Malden, MA: Blackwell Publishing Ltd.
Ellis, R. (1985). *Understanding second language acquisition.* Oxford: Oxford University Press.
Ellis, R. (2003). *Task-based language learning and teaching.* Oxford: Oxford University Press.
Fantini, A. E. (2000). A central concern: Developing intercultural competence. In A. E. Fantini (Ed.), *SIT occasional papers series: About our institution* (pp. 25–42). Brattleboro, VT: School for International Training.
Fennes, H., & Hapgood, K. (1997). *Intercultural learning in the classroom: Crossing borders.* London: Cassell Council of Europe Series.
Geertz, C. (1975). *The interpretation of cultures.* New York, NY: Basic Books.
Holliday, A., Hyde, M., & Kullman, J. (2004). *Inter-cultural communication: An advance resource book.* London: Routledge Applied Linguistics.
Hymes, D. (1972). On communicative competence. In J. P. Holmes (Ed.), *Sociolinguistics* (pp. 269–293). Harmondsworth: Penguin.
Idilkó, L., Huber-Kriegler, M., Lussier, D., Matei, G., & Peck, C. (2007). *Developing and assessing intercultural communicative competence.* Strasbourg: Council of Europe Publishing.
Kolb, D. (1984). *Experiential learning: Experience as the source of learning and development.* Englewood Cliffs, NJ: Prentice Hall.
Moon, A. J. (2004). *A handbook of reflective and experiential learning: Theory and practice.* Abingdon: RoutledgeFalmer.
Nunan, D. (1999). *Second language teaching.* Boston, MA: Heinle & Heinle Publishers.
Rico Martín, A. M. (2005). De la competencia intercultural en la adquisición de una segunda lengua o lengua extranjera: conceptos, metodologías y revisión de métodos. *Porta Linguarum, 3,* 79–94.
Rico-Troncoso, C. (2010). The effects of language materials on the development of intercultural competence. In B. Tomlinson & H. Masuhara (Eds.), *Research for materials development in language learning* (pp. 83–102). London: Continuum.
Savicki, V. (2008). *Developing intercultural competence and transformation: Theory, research and application in international education.* Sterling, VA: Stylus Publishing.
Sercu, L., Bandura, E., Castro, P., Davcheva, L., Laskaridou, C., Lundgren, U., del Carmen Méndes, G. M., & Ryan, P. (Eds.), *Foreign language teachers and intercultural competence: An international investigation.* Clevedon: Multilingual Matters.
Stern, H. (1983). *Fundamental concepts of language teaching.* Oxford: Oxford University Press.
Tomlinson, B. (2003). *Developing materials for language teaching.* London: Continuum.

Carlos Rico Troncoso
Languages Department
Pontificia Universidad Javeriana
Colombia

C. RICO-TRONCOSO

APPENDIX

Unit adapted from: Verdía, E., Fruns, J., Martín, F., Ortín, M., & Rodrigo, C. (2008). *En acción 2. Curso de español con enfoque orientado a la acción.* Spain: enCLAVE ELE.

Unidad 1   What do we know about ourselves?

OBJETIVO: Escribir un artículo con nuestras impresiones sobre el aprendizaje de una lengua.
Objective: Write an article about our impressions concerning learning a language

Coursebook: En Acción 2. Curso de Español con Enfoque Orientado a la Acción. Editorial En Clave ELE. España, 2008

¿Por qué nos cuesta tanto aprender idiomas? (p. 18)
Why do we find difficult to learn a language?

In this stage we re-engage with the text. This re-engagement lets us think of activities that stimulate students to think, reflect and communicate. With this thought in mind, we avoid adapting activities focused only on the linguistic features of the text.

ASSESSING INTERCULTURAL COMMUNICATIVE COMPETENCE

1. Observa lo que dicen estos estudiantes de español (Look at what these students of Spanish say)

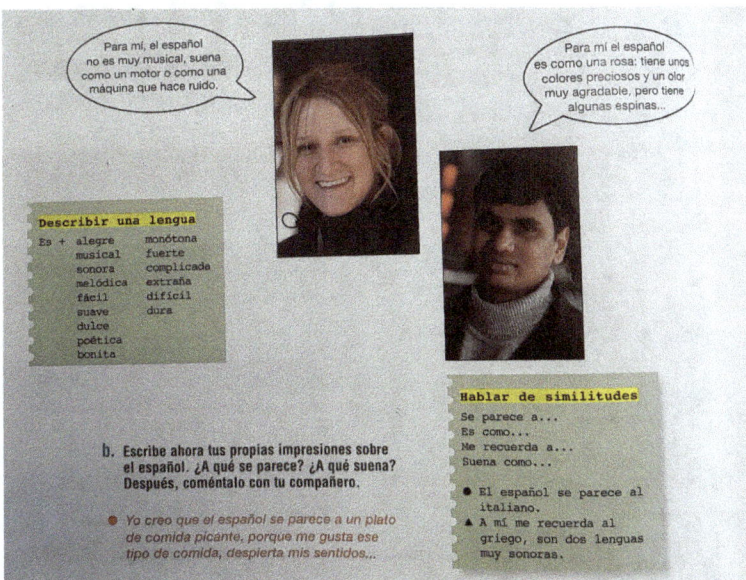

2. ¿Te llama la atención alguna de estas impresiones? ¿Cuál?/Is there any impression that calls your attention? Which one?
3. Comparte tu respuesta con tu compañero/Share your answer with your partner.
4. Escribe cinco palabras que describan tus impresiones sobre el español. ¿A qué suena? ¿A qué se parece?/Now write five words which describe your impressions about Spanish. What does this language sound like? What do you compare this language with?

5. Completa la siguiente tabla:/complete the following table

PREGUNTA	RESPUESTA
• ¿Qué idiomas hablas?	
• ¿Cuándo empezaste a aprenderlos?	
• ¿Por qué los aprendiste?	
• ¿Quieres aprender otra lengua? ¿Cuál?	

6. Ahora responde a este cuestionario sobre tus experiencias en las clases de idiomas./ Now complete this questionnaire about your experiences in your language classes.

TUS EXPERIENCIAS EN LAS CLASES DE IDIOMAS

1. Señala lo que más te ha ayudado a aprender en tus clases de idiomas.
   - ☐ Hablar y debatir temas en parejas o en grupos
   - ☐ Leer textos y responder a preguntas
   - ☐ Traducir textos
   - ☐ Escuchar una grabación y responder a preguntas
   - ☐ Escuchar al profesor
   - ☐ Escribir textos breves o sencillos (mensajes, postales...)
   - ☐ Escribir textos más complejos (redacciones, cartas...)
   - ☐ Hacer ejercicios gramaticales
   - ☐ Hacer juegos con la gramática, el vocabulario, etc.
   - ☐ Practicar la pronunciación
   - ☐ Hacer deberes y corregirlos
   - ☐ _____
   - ☐ _____

2. Señala qué prefieres hacer en clase (C) y qué fuera de clase (F).
   - ( ) Leer
   - ( ) Escribir
   - ( ) Hablar
   - ( ) Escuchar grabaciones
   - ( ) Hacer ejercicios de gramática
   - ( ) Hacer ejercicios de pronunciación
   - ( ) Memorizar listas de vocabulario
   - ( ) Aprender reglas de gramática
   - ( ) Buscar palabras nuevas en el diccionario
   - ( ) _____
   - ( ) _____

3. Normalmente, ¿cómo prefieres trabajar en el aula? (Señala una o varias opciones).
   - ☐ Solo/a
   - ☐ En parejas
   - ☐ En pequeños grupos
   - ☐ Con el profesor

4. ¿Cómo te sientes cuando, en clase, hablas la lengua que estudias? (Señala una o varias opciones).
   - ☐ Bastante seguro/a de mí mismo/a
   - ☐ Un poco incómodo/a
   - ☐ Como un/a niño/a pequeño/a
   - ☐ Siento un poco de vergüenza
   - ☐ No siento nada especial

5. ¿Qué es, para ti, lo más fácil del español?
   _____
   _____
   _____

6. ¿Y qué te cuesta hacer en español? Señálalo.
   - ☐ Aprender la gramática
   - ☐ Pronunciar bien (la _j_ o la _r_)
   - ☐ Hablar con fluidez
   - ☐ Recordar el vocabulario
   - ☐ Comprender conversaciones
   - ☐ Escribir correctamente
   - ☐ Leer textos complejos
   - ☐ _____
   - ☐ _____

7. ¿Qué es lo que más te gustó de tus anteriores clases de español (o de otras lenguas)?
   _____
   _____
   _____

8. ¿Y lo que menos?
   _____
   _____
   _____

7. Comparte tus respuestas con tu compañero/Share the answers with your partner

INTAKE RESPONSE ACTIVITIES

8. Vas a leer el artículo que ha publicado la revista **KWO** titulado *¿Por qué nos cuesta tanto aprender idiomas?*/You will read the article 'Why do we find difficult to learn a language' published by **KWO** Magazine

   Pero antes de leerlo, ¿Quién crees que ha escrito este artículo?/Before reading, think of who wrote this article?

9. ¿Cuál crees que sea el problema principal que se menciona en este artículo?/ What do you think is the main issue dealt with in this article?

ASSESSING INTERCULTURAL COMMUNICATIVE COMPETENCE

10. Ahora lee el artículo y compara tus respuestas./Now, read the article and compare your answers.

INPUT RESPONSE ACTIVITIES

Interpretation Tasks

11. Subraya en el texto dos problemas que tienen los estudiantes a la hora de aprender idiomas./Underline in the text, two problems students find when learning languages
12. Menciona dos ventajas de aprender un idioma distinto al materno./Mention two advantages of learning a language different from the mother tongue
13. Menciona dos problemas comunes que enfrentan los estudiantes al aprender un idioma./Mention two difficulties students find when learning a language

Awareness Tasks

14. ¿Cuál crees que es tu problema principal al aprender un idioma?/What do you think is the main difficulty you have when learning a language?
15. ¿Crees que los problemas que tienes son similares a los de otros aprendices de lenguas?/Do you think that your difficulties are similar to other language learners?
16. Piensa en un consejo que le darías a una persona que desea aprender un idioma./Think about an advice you would give to a person who is willing to learn a language

DEVELOPMENT ACTIVITIES

17. En grupos de tres van a hacer una entrevista a otro compañero sobre su aprendizaje de otra lengua. Las preguntas podrían ser:/In groups of three, you will interview one of your partners regarding his/her experiences about learning a language. Here there are some of questions that could help you with the interview.

- ¿Por qué aprendes español?
- ¿Qué es lo que más te gusta del español? ¿Y lo que menos?
- ¿Qué es lo que más te cuesta hacer en español?
- ¿Cómo te sientes cuando hablas español?
- ...

● Yo creo que también podemos preguntar qué hacen cuando están hablando y tienen una dificultad.
▲ De acuerdo. ¿Y cómo se pregunta eso en 2.ª persona singular?
■ Pues, «¿Qué haces cuando estás hablando y tienes una dificultad?»
▼ Sí, o «Cuando estás hablando, ¿cómo superas las dificultades?»

18. Cada uno se entrevista con un miembro de cada grupo y toma nota de sus respuestas. Each member of the group will interview another from a different group. Take notes of the answers given.
19. Regresa a tu grupo y pon en común los comentarios de los compañeros entrevistados para escribir un artículo como el de la revista *KWO*./Get back to your initial group and share the answers collected. You have to use this information to write an article for KWO Magazine.

LANGUAGE AND COMMUNICATION: Language forms and functions

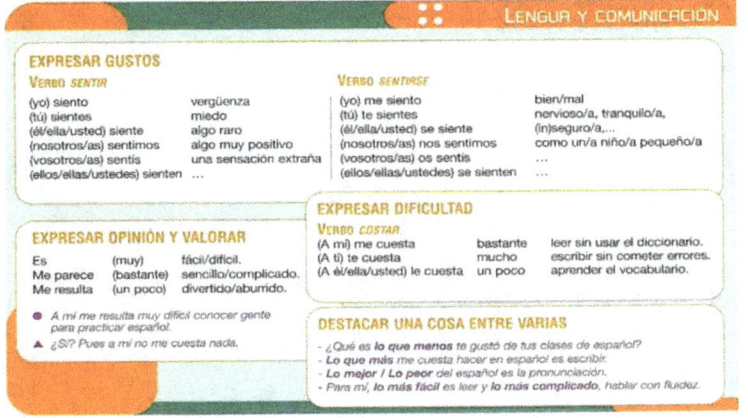

MARTIN CORTAZZI AND LIXIAN JIN

6. SOCIO-CULTURAL PERSPECTIVES ON COURSEBOOK EVALUATION

INTRODUCTION

In this chapter we first discuss key questions about socio-cultural perspectives to outline some fundamental evaluation criteria for TEFL coursebooks. We indicate a range of complexities which make this evaluation difficult without both global and local pedagogic considerations. Arguably, although socio-cultural features are sometimes separated out in specifically labelled cultural sections in coursebooks, in other ways these features are clearly integrated as inherent aspects of language use in what is presented to learners and in expected productive language activities. In worldwide uses of English this language-culture integration is perhaps most visible and increasingly common in intercultural communication (see Chapter 5). Thus although we separate out socio-cultural facets of coursebooks for purposes of analysis and discussion, we believe that in more holistically-oriented approaches to TEFL these facets will be well-integrated not only with language skills and activities but more broadly with intercultural skills and with critical and creative aspects of learning and using English. We emphasize a consideration of reflexivity – how evaluators, and classroom participants, need to consider not only 'target' cultures and social contexts around the English-speaking world but also to reflect on local societies and cultures, with which participants identify. Examples of such a holistic approach are given in relation to TEFL coursebooks for China.

SOCIO-CULTURAL ISSUES IN EVALUATION FROM A GLOBAL PERSPECTIVE

To 'evaluate' implies assessing the worth and value of something and making considered and balanced judgements about it, often using explicit criteria. In the case of evaluating social and cultural perspectives in EFL coursebooks this is problematic because we each bring our own social and cultural frameworks of values, experiences and beliefs to the evaluation. While this is true to some extent of any aspect of coursebook evaluation, it may be of greater impact for evaluating social and cultural features since teachers' professional training – and the literature about coursebook design and evaluation – often pays less attention to these aspects compared with the detail and depth given to considering teaching language skills, phonology, vocabulary or grammar. And yet, because language and cultural practices are intertwined and imperceptibly blended, social and cultural aspects are all-pervasive, whether a particular coursebook has highlighted them or not. Our own frameworks can, consciously or unwittingly, influence our perception of what the value and usefulness the socio-cultural content has for classrooms. Consideration of an evaluation framework should help to raise evaluators' awareness to minimize any negative or constraining aspects of this influence.

There is a range of theoretical perspectives relevant to textbooks and course materials. It is not necessarily obvious which perspectives on culture should be applied to coursebook design or avoided (e.g., see Figure 6.1). There is also a thorny practical choice of which cultures should or could be represented and which disciplinary perspectives are most useful (see Figure 6.2). This is rendered more complex by the obvious variety of English teaching and learning contexts around the world and hence of students' needs for socio-cultural aspects of learning in relation to their specific contexts. There is also some variety of English teachers' socio-cultural experiences and of their awareness of the contexts in which English is used. Worldwide, it is demanding for English teachers to be able to exploit the best materials with global knowledge and insights and yet be in a professional position to help learners with the details of socio-cultural features of cultures using English which can be compared with cultures familiar to particular groups of learners.

Such considerations raise a number of questions, including: who is evaluating, who are the learners intended for a given coursebook, which cultures are relevant, and – with some idea of selected social and cultural content – what kind of criteria are relevant for evaluation? The following sections are organised around these questions and provide contexts, discussion points and possible solutions.

Who Is Doing the Evaluation?

Evaluators may be policy makers, researchers, publishers, teacher trainers, trainees or experienced teachers, or students. We argue that in any evaluation, those carrying it out – or reading an evaluation report and review – need to consider their own social backgrounds, cultural identities and experiences, their allegiances or professional backgrounds in terms of academic disciplines, their knowledge and awareness of different societies and cultures around the world (see Figure 6.2). Thus evaluators first need to evaluate themselves. They need to try to make explicit to themselves their own presuppositions, expectations and principles of understanding cultures and societies which may be relevant to EFL pedagogy and to coursebooks. This is problematic because the socio-cultural knowledge which might be relevant to classroom teaching and using a coursebook is potentially apparently endless since it encompasses the cultures of the English-using world. Most evaluators will have individualized or locally influenced frameworks of understanding these issues. However, the key point here is for evaluators to ask reflexive questions about their own cultural background and social experience and link this with professional understanding of current trends in how different disciplines consider social and cultural contexts of language learning and use (see Figure 6.2).

Some perceptions of culture	Cautionary comments
Culture is an object	But culture is a process or inter-related networks of ways of interpreting meanings; otherwise this 'reification' makes a culture misleadingly into an object.
Culture is simple	But cultural processes are highly complex. In a pedagogic tendency to reduce a culture by ignoring internal variations, this 'reductionism' reduces complexity by over-simplifying to just a few characteristics.
Culture is uniform	But cultural communities inevitably include diversity and difference; not all individuals in a cultural group share the same characteristics; otherwise this 'essentialist' view misrepresents all members as sharing identical cultural characteristics, perhaps with a national label.
Culture is pure	But cultural authenticity is not necessarily confined to a particular period, source or place of origin, uninfluenced by other cultures; this 'homogenization' or 'uniformity' ignores mutual influences between cultures, cultural mixes, fusions, blends, and dynamic changes.
Culture is exotic	If other cultures are seen as strange or exotic, similarities or universal features are overlooked; this 'otherization' ignores individual variation and treats a group as 'Other', often with stereotyped labels.
Culture is fixed	But this 'stabilization' may ignore the dynamic nature of culture and current changes; although many cultural features change slowly, cultures should be seen as dynamic.
Culture is a nation	But few languages in the world can be identified with a single country or nation: with population movements, increasing diasporas and heritage communities, many cultures have become 'denationalized' or 'deterritorialized'. English is shared globally in many cultural communities.

Figure 6.1. Some perceptions of culture which from a global perspective are misaligned for representing 'target' cultures in TEFL coursebooks

This *reflexivity* is a kind of meta-reflection about one's own socio-cultural orientation and expectations within TEFL. Reflexivity is vital when coursebooks are evaluated as a teacher training activity since the objective of such training is not only to evaluate and consider how best to use given materials but to become more self-aware of the social and cultural presuppositions that are likely to influence the evaluation and therefore the classroom practices of those teaching socio-cultural features of the materials. Evaluation is a teacher development process. Evaluation is about ways of seeing and understanding what is in a coursebook but also concerns deepening our vision and frameworks of how to evaluate.

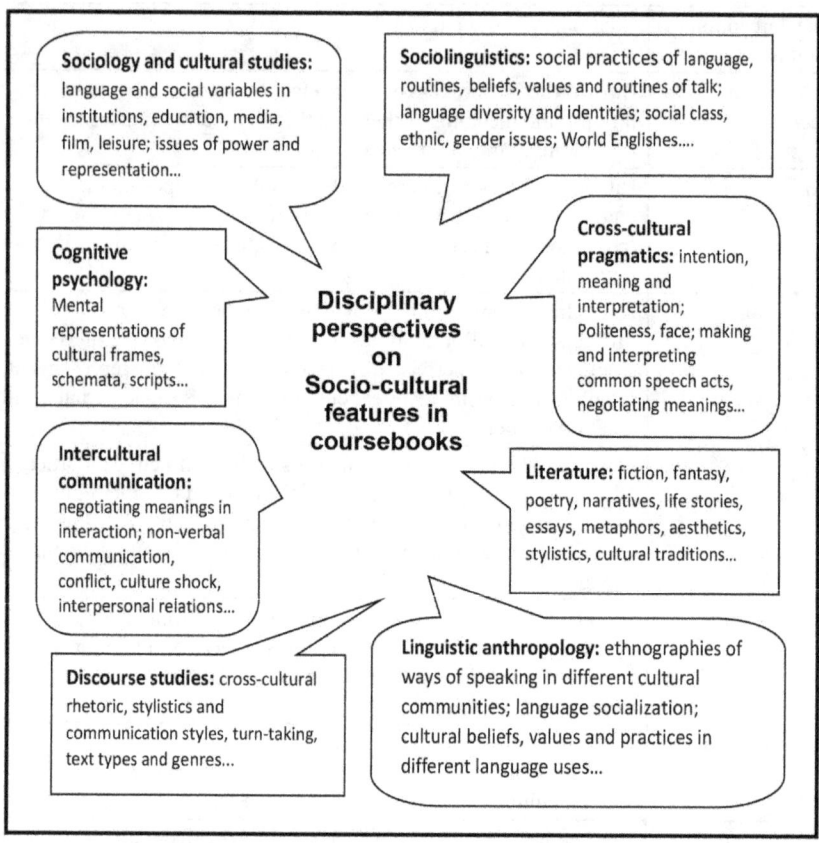

Figure 6.2. Some disciplinary perspectives giving conceptions of socio-cultural language use

Who Are the Learners? What Are Their Social and Cultural Backgrounds? What Are Their Purposes and Needs in Relation to the Coursebook?

The learners' direct access to social and cultural experience of using English and interacting with skilled speakers depends in part on whether the learning situation is broadly ESL or EFL. In EFL situations the learners' access to social interaction with competent users and with the media is generally far more limited. This means the coursebook materials and teachers may be the main source of direct socio-cultural information and vicarious experience through activities. In ESL situations, learners likely have some access to uses of the target language in their own society, so coursebooks may be designed as a bridge to social engagement with English in local situations.

Cutting across these distinctions, in many contemporary urban contexts there is increasingly social and cultural diversity because of population movements. Diversity affects conceptions of 'target' social contexts (in terms of racial, ethnic, religious, linguistic and cultural diversity) but it also means that some groups of learners themselves already represent a rich diversity of cultural experience which varies from one group of students to another or between individuals. Thus learners of English in London – an obvious 'target culture' city – may experience the 'superdiversity' of a city where over 300 languages are spoken and over 20% of the multicultural residents use English as a second language; this is a different cultural experience compared to that of learners in Beijing, Jakarta, Istanbul or Prague where diversity is much less obvious.

In any case, the coursebook can develop the reflexive principle that to develop socio-cultural understanding and relevant language skills also requires learners to analyze and reflect on their own situations and their own uses of their first or other languages (not only of English). This is a well-recognized major principle of cultural teaching in TEFL: it should include a key element that learners reflect on and articulate explicitly aspects of their own cultural heritages and social practices. Applying this principle is a useful educational aim in its own right and it assists and supports the development of socio-cultural skills in English.

This principle of reflexivity, then, relates to the evaluator, and also to teachers' and learners' actual pedagogic uses of EFL materials, and therefore as a basic principle of socio-cultural learning it is also a key question for evaluating coursebooks: *How (and in what ways, how far, and how well) is reflexivity embodied in the coursebook?* This reflexivity should enable teachers and learners to be aware of, know and understand key features of societies, cultures and contexts around the world in which English has a major use and at the same time systematically know and understand their own social and cultural contexts through comparison, discussion and reflective thinking.

Which Cultures Are Relevant?

There seem to be four stages of development of perceptions in answering this question. Some national education systems or particular institutions may be at different stages, while international publishers of coursebooks clearly identify themselves with later stages, so these stages have influenced coursebook choices.

In a first stage, 'target cultures' were exclusively or largely confined to those national contexts where English was used by perceived 'native speakers' (e.g. USA, UK, or Australia). This was largely the case up to the 1980s. However, in the education systems of some countries although the target language was English, the cultures featured in national textbooks were those of the students' home or 'source' cultures and not those of English speakers (see examples in Cortazzi & Jin, 1999). Some national policies held that learners should be able to talk about their own society and culture to visitors in English. However, there was sometimes an asymmetry: English-using cultures, especially those of native-speaking societies perceived as globally dominant (e.g., USA), were not featured in some textbooks, implicitly because they were seen as a threat to local cultures and identities (Cortazzi & Jin, 1999). However, it should go without elaboration that learning about other cultures and societies through ELT need not be a threat to local identity but may enhance it; in many places both target and local cultures were included.

More generally in a second stage from the 1990s, the focus on 'target' cultures widened beyond obvious native-speaking contexts to include an increasing international range of cultural contexts where English is a major national second language (e.g., India, Singapore) or where bilingual education includes English (e.g. South Africa, Lebanon, or Brunei). This broadening conception of 'World English' can be seen to include a huge number of linguistic varieties (Davies, 2005; McArthur, 2002) although there has been a considerable lag in working out how this could or should affect cultural aspects of coursebook design. Further recognition includes contexts where English has a strong role in higher education (e.g., Malaysia, Finland, or Germany) as an international university lingua franca (Jenkins, 2014) or even a major foreign language. Potentially this comprises a huge number of national, professional, business and leisure contexts where English is used.

In a third stage from the early 2000s, the increasing awareness of English as a transnational medium of communication in the media, the internet, international conferences, or business meetings means that speakers of English bring the cultural ways of speaking, knowledge and experiences of practically any society or community world-wide into their English usage. It is therefore fully justified to consider for coursebooks any socio-cultural context of 'World Englishes' or 'Global Englishes' (Jenkiins, 2015; Kirkpatrick, 2007; Schneider, 2011). This perspective includes the cultures of native-speakers of English, but also cultures where English is used by second language users or learners of English. In principle, any and all cultures of the globe are relevant, since speakers from any of these cultural contexts may be using English with other speakers from any other English-using cultural community. In practice, this global perspective should include some examples of minority cultures within larger societies and also local cultures of learners: this gives the opportunity for learners to reflect on the more familiar in new ways and facilitates meaningful comparisons within and across particular contexts. Balancing global and local perspectives has implications for using international coursebooks or more local materials.

In practice a given coursebook cannot handle more than a representative range of cultures for reasons of limited space, teaching-learning time, and constraints on authors' expertise. A feasible selection depends on consideration of materials writers', teachers' and learners' knowledge, experience, likely interests, and other considerations of relevance, such as neighbouring cultures within a region, social situations of likely communication for education, travel and tourism, migration, trade and international relations.

In a fourth stage, which overlaps with stage three from the late 1990s, ELT programmes, and therefore coursebook designers, have gradually been developing conceptions of *intercultural communication,* seeing intercultural learning as a valid and vital educational aim in its own right (Byram, 1997; Byram et al., 2001; Corbett, 2003, 2010; Fennes & Hapgood, 1997). Rather than simply considering language with cultural content and context, intercultural skills are emphasized (Hua, 2014; Jackson, 2014). Social awareness, cultural knowledge and understanding, interactional and communication skills and problem-solving are developed in relation to example intercultural contexts so that learners are prepared linguistically and socially to engage productively with any cultural context and manage an orientation to learning interculturally. This perspective includes socio-cultural contexts of the learners themselves, but here the reflexivity is applied to solving intercultural issues in which their own practices are relevant. Arguably, this intercultural communication cannot be developed educationally unless cultural learning is linked to a creative approach to handle novelty, difference, diversity, and a critical approach which develops the necessary mindfulness and problem-solving stance towards learning – these are educational aims in their own right (Cortazzi & Jin, 2004, 2013).

Implied additional questions here are: *what views of culture are relevant? What do we mean by 'culture'?* Likely discussion behind these questions can raise issues of stereotyping, essentialism and reification and related themes (see Figure 6.1). Arguably a contemporary coursebook should not only avoid such misconceptions of 'culture' but might take active steps through activities to counteract them. Teachers would be alert for student thinking about 'their culture' or 'our culture', which may suggest stereotypes, and especially to help learners avoid *'ethnocentrism'* (seeing the world only from the view of one's own people, and supposing that one's own groups' standards are superior and implying other groups are inferior).

What Kinds of Criteria Are Considered Relevant for Evaluation?

If evaluation criteria are imposed from outside a given teaching context, they may be mediated or filtered in practice by participants' personal and social backgrounds. On the other hand, if only personal and local criteria are used, this may deprive participants of pedagogic thinking, which is an unnecessary barrier for professional development and culture learning and engagement.

Our list of criteria comes largely from our own professional practices in international contexts, influenced by classic writers on materials and culture (e.g., Byram, 1997; Byrd, 1995; Cunningsworth, 1995; Gray, 2002; McDonough & Shaw, 1993; McGrath, 2002; Tomlinson, 1998, 2003, 2008).

An over-arching criterion for evaluating socio-cultural aspects of TEFL coursebooks is *pedagogic validity* – the extent to which coursebook contents and related activities reflect and represent societies and cultures in realistic ways and engage learners practically in systematic and worthwhile teaching and learning. This can be expanded with details:

- *Conceptions of society and culture:* the explicit or implicit conceptions of society and culture which emerge in both contents and designed learning processes; how far any misleading ideas about cultures are evident or counteracted (see Figure 6.1).
- *Disciplinary perspectives:* the theoretical frameworks deriving from academic disciplines which underlie features and representations of societies and cultures and pedagogic activities (see Figure 6.2).
- *Selection:* the choices of socio-cultural features in coursebook contents and processes of use which are appropriate to given groups of participants; this recognizes that length is limited and that often much coursebook content is pre-specified by a syllabus; this might be extended by ideas of *socio-moral legitimacy,* where choices should be sensitive to particular social, moral, religious or political contexts.
- *Authenticity:* the inclusion of realistic contexts and cultural situations; this might be extended to *veridicality* to allow for fiction, history, fantasy or poetry which would have the ring of truth related to believable mental and emotional lives.
- *Representation:* the extent to which selected features are reasonably representative of societies and cultures; this should avoid stereotypes and over-generalizations and indicate differences and exceptions to what is presented; this would also be extended to *socio-cultural diversity* and *inclusivity*, which refers to the extent that different age groups, genders, minority groups in society, family types, social backgrounds or occupations are included.
- *Relevance:* the extent to which materials are relevant to specific groups of learners and their situation, language level, previous study, interests; apparently exotic or remote materials can be made relevant by simple introductions or adaptations; this can be related to *accessibility*, to the extent to which extracts, scenes and slices of events and materials can be accessed by learners without extensive background information.
- *Integration:* the extent to which social and cultural issues are integrated into texts, language activities and practice exercises; this seems more natural and productive, but it does not prevent highlighting specific points (e.g., in 'Culture Notes'), or deny the usefulness of specific cultural readings or activities.
- *Engagement:* the interest, liveliness, thoughtfulness, and humour, through which learners participate mentally, emotionally and socially to sustain activities, and linked to *reflexivity*; this might be extended to *social commitment* to promote thinking about and discussing serious issues and engage learners in appropriate aspects of philosophy, morality, social life and citizenship and limit trivial or banal content in favour of educational depth; further extension can be thought of as *worthwhileness* – the extent to which, through language development, coursebook contents and processes have educational value to develop learners' thinking, imagination, critical understanding and ideas about living a worthwhile life.
- *Potential for exploitation:* the extent to which the content, task design, instructions and suggested follow-up activities enable learners potentially and

where appropriate to take learning beyond what is explicit in a Students' Book; this could include alternatives, extensions, applications to out-of-class activities, projects or presentations for social and cultural comparison; this may include academic or social *challenge*; suggestions might be outlined in a Teacher's Book.

Stages	Comments from socio-cultural perspectives
Pre-use	*Purpose:* to evaluate to choose or approve materials at a design stage before they are published or prior to classroom use; *Socio-cultural issues:* What is the stance of the designers and authors on these issues? How is this stance informed theoretically and professionally? What themes and topics are relevant, interesting and feasible to teach? How far will activities engage learners in discussion and thinking? Are there a representative variety of social and cultural contexts and issues? How do learners build up a picture of world-wide contexts of using English? How are social and cultural aspects integrated with language features? How will the material facilitate meaningful reflection on learners' own local and national cultures beside those of English-speakers?
In-use	*Purpose:* to observe and ascertain the actual use of materials with learners in class and see what kinds of interaction participants are engaged in, to observe particular kinds of learners or how supplementary materials of Teacher's Books are used. *Socio-cultural issues:* How do teachers and students actually use the materials in ways that consistently help to develop social and cultural awareness with intercultural skills? What is the range of strategies for teaching and learning embodied in the materials? Is the guidance and support from the Teacher's Book or supplementary materials being drawn upon effectively? How are students seen to be engaged in socio-cultural issues in different activities?
Post-use	*Purpose:* to evaluate to improve the impact and effectiveness of materials on student learning; to improve learning processes or to revise the materials; *Socio-cultural issues:* What assessment strategies are used to evaluate the impact of teaching and learning on students' awareness, knowledge, understanding, and communication skills in relation to different contexts and interaction with English speakers from different backgrounds? What feedback and comments do students and teachers give on social and cultural features of the materials?

Figure 6.3. Some stages of evaluation of socio-cultural aspects of TEFL materials

There are several caveats with such criteria. First, the list can be extended; yet the more detailed the list becomes, the more idealized it appears and the more challenging it becomes to embody such features. Second, criteria work together: in practice they might be variously combined in a holistic *pedagogic validity*. Third, the realization of criteria in coursebooks is not only in reading or listening texts, but might be enacted multi-modally through illustrations, sound recordings, video extracts, cultural notes, sidebars, explanations and glosses, and of course through participants' activity and interaction such as in role plays and prepared presentations.

One approach to evaluation, drawing on the above criteria, is to follow the common stages for designing and enacting activities for reading with texts (pre-reading, while-reading, post-reading). This distinguishes three stages, as in Figure 6.3. A useful approach or teacher training and postgraduate TEFL courses is to go systematically through a coursebook to find and assess representations under various headings which comprise different disciplinary perspectives which are current in applied linguistics (see Figure 6.2); each of these can help evaluators to assess features and to highlight awareness of how different perspectives might be realized in practice. We give a pragmatics example later.

EVALUATING COURSEBOOKS IN CHINA

As a case study, we consider evaluating the socio-cultural perspectives embodied in ELT coursebooks which are written to align with the national *College English* syllabus for students in China. This is an important case, since China has more learners of English than any other country. In recent years, skills in a foreign language, predominantly English, have been assessed by a national College English test often as a requirement for university graduation but many students study to pass more advanced levels of the test to gain advantages for professional employment.

We refer to four series of materials for *College English* courses published in China jointly by Macmillan with Shanghai Foreign Language Education Press (Smallwood et al., 2002, 2004, 2005, henceforth referred to as 'the Shanghai coursebooks') and with the Foreign Language Teaching and Research Press in Beijing (Greenall et al., 2009a, 2009b, 2012, referred to here as 'the Beijing coursebooks'). These series are specially written by teams of British and Chinese authors. They are currently in press for a second edition. With each publisher, there are two series (respectively emphasizing integrated skills, and listening and speaking) each with four levels of Students' Books and accompanying Teacher's Books. There are discs with audio recordings for pronunciation and listening to dialogues. The Beijing coursebooks have discs of video recordings: some are scripted and acted on location, modelling Chinese and British/American participants in interaction; others are extracts from authentic recordings of presentations and interactions. There are also Cultural Readers of matching levels, a Student Workbook, and, for teachers, access to purpose-written internet activities for lesson planning and additional follow-up material as teacher resources and for assessment purposes.

We have been closely involved with designing these as the series editor, cultural editor and authors for the Shanghai coursebooks, and as authors of accompanying Teacher's Books for the Beijing coursebooks. This involvement with these coursebooks may make an evaluation less impartial than seems desirable. However, in education, including ELT, it is commonplace for teachers to evaluate their own work. And reflection and reflexivity are widely held as markers of professional engagement in professional development or research (Edge, 2011).

Looking at the Beijing coursebooks first, some idea of the geographical, historical, artistic and social range of contexts can be gauged from the themes of *authentic video extracts* which include homes in Britain, the 16th century British queen Elizabeth I, surprising aspects of Australia, cooking in an American ethnic minority style in Louisiana, women in South Korea, Asian holidays and customs, online shopping, students doing voluntary work, job interviews, school research on happiness, and critical comments on the Italian artist Leonardo da Vinci's portrait of the Mona Lisa. This shows that while obvious 'Western' cultures are included the topics also relate to minority groups or social issues, and that cultures, customs and socio-educational themes also comprise both Asian regional settings and technical and social developments in, potentially, any global location.

This impression is greatly reinforced by considering the content themes of *'Reading across Cultures'*, a one-page text section with discussion questions which is designed to support the two main texts with socio-cultural dimensions related to the unit theme. These include features on specific aspects of the USA (summer camps for young people, games people play, Santa Fe city in New Mexico state), Western traditions and developments – not necessarily in English-speaking contexts (street markets in the UK, France, Germany and Austria; banknote designs in the EU; the top five paintings in Western art; migration into Europe from north Africa; heroes in Western literature; Aesop's fables), and some examples of specifically non-English speaking cultural events and issues which exemplify what some may consider minority perspectives on international living (celebrating indigenous festivals in Mexico, Inuit legends in Greenland, the Nigerian writer Chinua Achebe's writing in English, saunas for health in Finland, preserving the Icelandic language). Examples of features which are specifically subtitled 'around the world' suggest a global remit of intercultural communication in English and include: customs related to falling in love, rites of passage, street food, the printed press, number sayings and proverbs, smiling, gestures, and thinking skills. Themes which may concern students' perceptions of commitments for change include: feminism in the last fifty years, the work of the International Red Cross and Red Crescent, and eco-tourism.

In the above sections there are systematic discussion points for students to consider the theme in relation to Chinese social contexts and to make comparisons with their local and national cultures in China. The Teachers' Books suggest solutions to problems posed and possible student responses to questions: these are designed consistently to exemplify likely Chinese experiences and viewpoints but to expand these with appreciation of the international social and cultural content and sometimes comments on developing identities (many teachers share these examples with classes electronically).

This design to develop reflexivity is more thoroughly applied in the *Cultural Readers*, supplementary books which are coordinated with themes for each level and contain many illustrated one-paragraph explanations of linguistic and cultural references in texts (Greenall et al., 2012). In particular, each unit has two one-page 'Culture Focus' texts on parallel culturally-related topics. Crucially, most of these invite reflexivity because whatever the topic of the first text (it is generally western or internationally oriented), the second comments on Chinese parallel cases (see examples in Figure 6.4). Each has three or four discussion questions asking for comments, personal reactions and opinions; often these stimulate a deeper level of thinking and they include specific points to think about cultures and identities around the world and in China. In a critical view, this Chinese socio-cultural comparison can be overdone and may be reduced to a routine, but it accords with current national policies.

Culture Focus 1	Culture Focus 2
Higher education in Brazil	China's higher education boom
A conversation about learning styles	Chinese philosophy: three great influential thinkers
Migration and social integration	'Foreigners' doing business in China
Shopping using mobile devices and the internet	Following the ancient merchants' Silk Road in China
Family commitments	*Family Instructions*, a 4th century Chinese classic text
The measure of a real hero: role model celebrities	Heroism across cultures: Chinese literary classics
Mud baths: ancient health benefits around the world	Ancient Chinese medical sciences for modern illnesses
Jane Austen and romance literature	The butterfly lovers: a Chinese 'Romeo and Juliet' story
Stendhal syndrome: a medical condition of being overwhelmed by art	Chinese art: how is it different?
Eating out in Britain	Culinary delights in China
Greek and Chinese myths	The mythic origin of the Mid-Autumn Chinese festival
An inconvenient truth: world-wide environmental issues in an American perspective	The Three Gorges modern dam in China: a struggle between man and nature?
Cross-cultural naming traditions	Naming practices in China

Figure 6.4. Developing cultural comparison, reflexivity and identity through parallel culture focus sections of cultural readers (topics in Greenall et al., 2012)

A critical point is that the efficacy of such reading texts ultimately depends on the students' use of them in discussing themes, and in extending their understanding through imagining further examples and applications. The main coursebook design attempts to handle this through the *Unit Tasks*, which are end-of-unit activities for learners in groups to apply thematic content personally for posters, presentations and

Preparing a shopping guide for your town	Writing a guide for foreign visitors on how to communicate in China
Writing an encyclopaedia entry about sports in China	Proposing ideas for a language reform
Preparing a presentation about a war	Designing a volunteer project
Carrying out a survey about students' experience of crime	Writing a 'Did you know?' article with facts from science
Promoting a community arts event	Defending a traditional job or trade in the modern world
Holding a meeting about an environmental issue	Writing a calendar of Chinese festivals with explanatory notes
Giving visitors advice about local food	Presenting your list of the top five things to read
Holding a press conference	Producing a leaflet on places of artistic interest
Writing a campus guide for international students in your university in China	Preparing a guide for immigrants to China

Figure 6.5. Socio-cultural features observable in unit tasks for student activities (in Greenall et al., 2008–2009)

similar classroom events (see Figure 6.5). Students are given guidance for structuring and presenting such tasks. The Teacher's Book has examples of completed tasks, generally including further social and cultural insights.

A further critical point is that much of the effective realization of these materials must depend on teachers' professional training. In China, this is problematic regarding socio-cultural aspects of TEFL because apart from literature perspectives these rarely feature strongly in training programmes even at postgraduate level. To support teachers, therefore, sections of the Teacher's Book are specifically designed for teacher development. These include explanations for activities, extensive cultural notes in the main coursebooks and in the Culture Reading books, plus additional or alternative ways to use activities. Yet further tasks appear in the Teacher's Books in the format of *photocopiable worksheets*, each with an introductory rationale and explanation and each with suggested solutions and responses to tasks. Many concern discourse approaches to teaching text organization, e.g. for evaluating argumentation, others link historical features of language with culture, including such topics as: Greek and Roman mythology, Shakespeare and the English language, Latin and Greek roots in English vocabulary, the language of music to describe instruments and musical performance, and metaphors using the language of cooking, food and taste.

Turning to the Shanghai coursebooks, parallel examples show a huge range of social and cultural themes, contexts and issues, including: mixed race marriages, experiences of physical disabilities, World Englishes, languages and communication in Australia, exams across cultures, asking questions in education across cultures, and gift giving across cultures (with Intercultural Notes giving detailed explanations for some of these). A section in each unit on 'Expanding your Creativity' encourages oral expression ways which differ from both traditional and recent activities in Chinese ELT (Cortazzi & Jin, 2013). Each activity is by definition different from all others, but each asks students in pairs or groups to actively use English in new contexts in ways that go beyond accuracy and fluency. They emphasize interest, imagination, visualizing alternatives, engaging in problem-solving, using judgement or applying personal and social values (see examples in Figure 6.6). Creative tasks include prioritizing new facilities for the disabled, evaluating qualities relating to loving relationships, writing songs or poems featuring the interpretation of colours across cultures, or making up slogans related to fitness and healthy living. These activities lead to oral presentations in class, with a rationale. To develop critical appreciation, these books gradually introduce communication criteria to evaluate presentations and help teachers give explicit feedback to learners. Later, after students have had the opportunity to internalize this process, teachers hand over this evaluation process to learners. Students draw up and apply their own criteria, including criteria of intercultural communication, e.g. that this should be appropriate, efficient, effective, and satisfying (Ting-Toomey, 1999).

Further socio-cultural applications are seen in a 'Culture Corner' in each unit (designed by Jin), which raises issues that have been observed to be problematic for Chinese learners of English in intercultural face-to-face interactions in China and internationally. The section shows how particular verbal events can be interpreted or misinterpreted by participants in cross-cultural pragmatics (see Figure 6.2): this can lead to wrong impressions, misunderstandings or mistaken evaluations of people which can reinforce stereotypes (examples of topics are given in Figure 6.7). Different cultural viewpoints are illustrated with cartoons, and the activity encourages students to observe and analyse interactions themselves by showing what features of context, cultural frameworks, interaction and language to look out for.

'Culture Corners' are each followed by a 'Participation Activity'. This highlights an observed intercultural communication situation or significant incident which has different cultural interpretations which can lead to misinterpretations, misperceptions, or conflict. Learners are presented with different choices for action or interpretation; they discuss and choose one which they feel is most appropriate, with reasons, and consider the consequences of other choices and who might make these other choices (see Cushner & Brislin, 1997). We call this a 'Participation Activity' to emphasize that students need to talk about and often re-enact or role play such situations. There are no right or wrong answers, but through the Teacher's Book students are given further notes on the 'Culture Corner', with key questions to help them consider the 'Participation Activity' situations in more depth, and feedback comments for each choice. Thus the main point of the activity is to consider and verbalize interactional choices, imagine and discuss alternative cultural consequences and cross-cultural

- put qualities for a successful personal relationship in rank order, from a given list (e.g. romance, honour, trust, family background, wealth, loyalty, accommodation)
- design a tee shirt with a message to express your thinking about a local environmental issue
- decide what money means most to people in your group (e.g. security, power, happiness, comfort, health and well-being, family status, property ownership)
- design a poster to advertise and recommend a newly issued book, song, or film
- interpret some intercultural data about good students and comment on its significance and interest for your group
- design an event for the 'Verbal Olympics': all events must emphasize people's verbal abilities (e.g. telling jokes or stories, presenting introductions, arguments and speeches ... the longest/shortest/most moving/most entertaining/most expressive/most informative ...)
- make 'guidelines for the guides', i.e. 'Dos and Don'ts' for Chinese guides to interact with international visitors and tourists (e.g. explaining, sustaining interest, entertaining, organizing a group, time-keeping, visitors' cultural values)
- prioritize facilities for town planning in your locality (e.g. shopping, businesses, sports & leisure, entertainments, scenic landscaping, transport, tourist and visitor facilities, environmental aspects)
- write and perform a dialogue between a young person in love and their parents (who think their son/daughter is being unwise)

Figure 6.6. Examples of activities to develop creativity in social contexts in pairs and groups for classroom presentations (Smallwood et al., 2002, 2004, 2005)

In different cultures, there may be different ways of speaking and interpreting social interaction seen through ...	
- cultural ways of listening - expressing disagreement - giving and accepting invitations - indicating preferences - persuading others - praising yourself - ways of presenting arguments - presenting balanced arguments - asking questions in formal contexts - politeness using mobile phones	- asking when you are not sure - using intonation to express meaning - expressing feelings and emotions - cultural views of classroom interaction - managing culture shock and changes - linguistic aspects of competitiveness - topics for chatting socially - expressing humour - politeness with emails - expressing appreciation

Figure 6.7. Raising awareness of politeness practices across culture (Smallwood et al., 2004, 2005)

explanations of politeness, and to role play similar scenarios – all in English. Figure 6.8 shows three stages of Participation Activities.

Together, the three stages (in Figure 6.8) give students considerable practice to develop their intercultural awareness with a critical-creative approach which

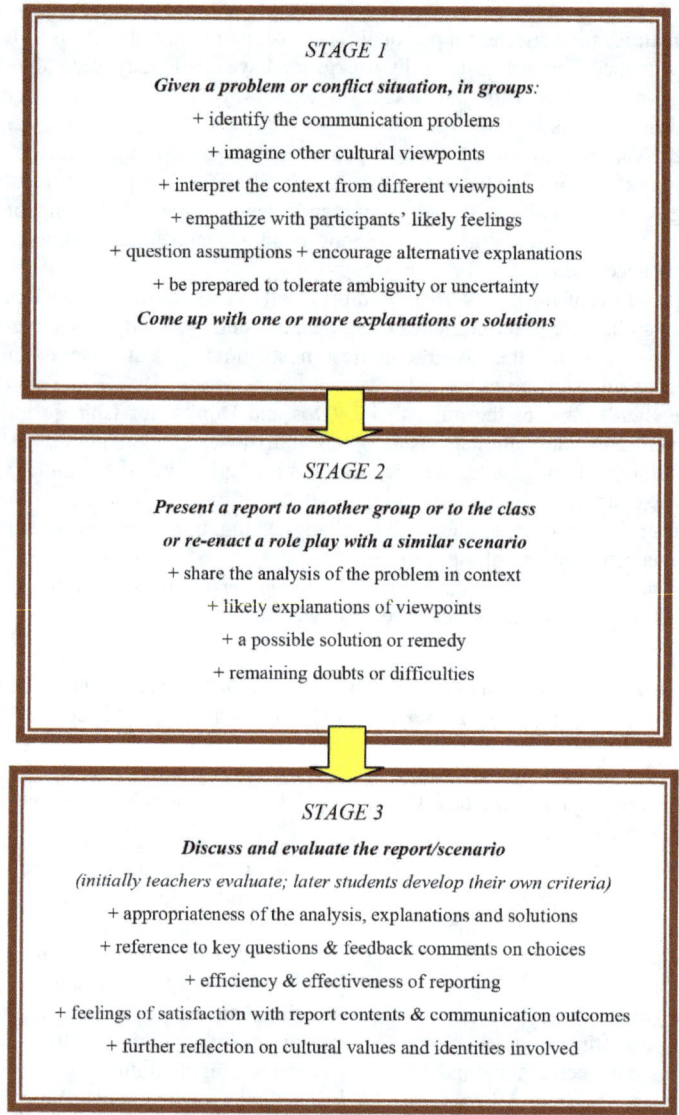

Figure 6.8. Three stages of participation activities to develop reflexivity in intercultural communication skills (based on Smallwood et al., 2002, 2004, 2005)

considers different social views, experiences and feelings. While this is a consistent cross-cultural pragmatic perspective throughout the Shanghai coursebooks, arguably other perspectives (in Figure 6.2) should be equally developed: they are observable in some units but are less obvious.

CONCLUSION

The case study of these EFL coursebooks for China exemplifies close attention to *pedagogic validity* in socio-cultural perspectives and we give brief conclusions about the application of our more detailed evaluation criteria to this case.

Pedagogic validity is clearly seen in the *selection* of social and cultural contexts which demonstrate systematic choices within all four of the cultural stages we outlined earlier. *Authenticity* is visible in authentic video extracts in the Beijing materials and *veridicality* is salient in these and in the Shanghai materials, where in both cases coursebooks are specially written and edited by Sino-British teams of contemporary expert writers. In both Beijing and Shanghai materials there could perhaps be greater *representation* of cultural diversity and social inclusivity, both internationally and within Chinese contexts: we have illustrated how writers certainly pay attention to this aspect and we note that in Chinese contexts this angle of socio-cultural perspectives is novel in ELT materials and that the Teacher's Books do develop this further. *Relevance* seems to saturate the Beijing materials and is also deeply embedded in those from Shanghai: clearly this is a major strength in these ELT materials for China. A further strength is the *integration* of socio-cultural perspectives with developing language skills. Both the Beijing and Shanghai materials appropriately highlight the cultural aspects in the coursebook introductions. Regarding *exploitability,* this again seems high in both sets of materials: this is evident in the classroom practicality of tasks and activities. The Teacher's Books indicate further dimensions with extra classroom ideas and applications which allow for some diversity of learning contexts within China (e.g. to provide both extra challenges for more able learners and to give ideas for easier access for learners with less experience of learning English).

We have highlighted the theme of *reflexivity*, not only for students but also for teachers: this is conspicuous in social and cultural comparisons, especially in the Beijing materials, and it is systematically developed in an innovative way in the Participation Activities in the Shanghai coursebooks. Some critics might look for greater social *engagement* regarding contemporary global issues: we have shown how the Beijing materials engage learners with some issues (e.g., the environment, migration, health), as do the Shanghai coursebooks. Of course, other issues which seem desirable to discuss from social equality viewpoints in 'the west' may not be appropriate to Chinese ideas and policies of *socio-moral legitimacy.* We can note how the second edition updates some aspects, e.g. the Shanghai coursebooks feature such topics as the banking crisis, entrepreneurship, personal counselling, and extending students' work and life experience.

Finally, we note how the Beijing coursebooks have unit sections on 'Developing Critical Thinking' and the Teacher's Books have teacher development sections on academic discourse skills, e.g. on argumentation. In complementation, the Shanghai coursebooks have unit sections on 'Expanding Your Creativity' promoting imaginative uses of English with examples in the Teacher's Books. In our own perspectives on socio-cultural issues in coursebook design we put high value on the integration of critical and imaginative thinking with developing social and cultural uses of English. We think of the conjunction of developing social and cultural skills with critical and creative approaches in global awareness as essential to meet the criterion of *worthwhileness*. This helps make TEFL coursebooks a key part of human and humane education.

REFERENCES

Byram, M. (1997). *Teaching and assessing intercultural communicative competence*. Clevedon: Multilingual Matters.
Byram, M., Nichols, A., & Stevens, D. (Eds.). (2001). *Developing intercultural competence in practice*. Clevedon: Multilingual Matters.
Byrd, P. (Ed.). (1995). *Materials writers' guide*. New York, NY: Heinle & Heinle.
Corbett, J. (2003). *An intercultural approach to English language teaching*. Clevedon: Multilingual Matters.
Corbett, J. (2010). *Intercultural language activities*. Cambridge: Cambridge University Press.
Cortazzi, M., & Jin, L. (1999). Cultural mirrors: Materials and methods in the EFL classroom. In E. Hinkel (Ed.), *Culture in second language teaching and learning* (pp. 196–220). Cambridge: Cambridge University Press.
Cortazzi, M., & Jin, L. (2004). Orientations to cultural engagement in ELT materials. In S. Rafik-Galea (Ed.), *ELT teaching materials: Theory and practice* (pp. 35–53). Petaling Jaya: Sasbadi Holdings Berhad.
Cortazzi, M., & Jin, L. (2013). Creativity and criticality: Developing dialogues of learning and thinking through synergy with China. In T. Coverdale-Jones (Ed.), *Transnational higher education in the Asian context* (pp. 97–117). Houndmills: Palgrave Macmillan.
Cunningsworth, A. (1995). *Choosing your coursebook*. Oxford: Macmillan Heinemann.
Cushner, K., & Brislin, R. W. (Eds.). (1997). *Improving intercultural interactions, modules for cross-cultural training programs*. Thousand Oaks: Sage Publications.
Davies, D. (2005). *Varieties of modern English, an introduction*. Harlow: Pearson Longman.
Edge, J. (Ed.). (2011). *The reflexive educator in TESOL, roots and wings*. London: Routledge.
Fennes, H., & Hapgood, K. (1997). *Intercultural learning in the classroom*. London: Cassell.
Gray, J. (2002). The global coursebook in English language teaching. In D. Block & D. Cameron (Eds.), *Globalization and language teaching* (pp. 151–167). London: Routledge.
Greenall, S., Wen, Q.-F., Newbold, D., & Friedland, D. (2009a). *Real communication, an integrated course* (Books 1, 2, 3, 4). Beijing: Macmillan/Foreign Language Teaching and Research Press.
Greenall, S., Wen, Q.-F., Tomalin, M., & Friedland, D. (2009b). *Real communication, listening and speaking* (Books 1, 2, 3, 4). Beijing: Macmillan/Foreign Language Teaching and Research Press.
Greenall, S., Wen Q.-F., Leung, L. K., Newbold, D., & Gao, H. (2012). *Real communication culture reading* (Books 1, 2, 3, 4). Beijing: Macmillan/Foreign Language Teaching and Research Press.
Hua, Z. (2014). *Exploring intercultural communication, language in action*. London: Routledge.
Jackson, J. (2014). *Introducing language and intercultural communication*. London: Routledge.
Jenkins, J. (2014). *English as a lingua franca in the international university: The politics of academic English language policy*. Abingdon: Routledge.
Jenkins, J. (2015). *Global Englishes: A resource book for students* (3rd ed.). Abingdon: Routledge.
Kirkpatrick, A. (2007). *World Englishes: Implications for international communication and English language teaching*. Cambridge: Cambridge University Press.
McArthur, T. (2002). *Oxford guide to world English*. Oxford: Oxford University Press.
McDonough, J., & Shaw, C. (1993). *Materials and methods in ELT*. Oxford: Blackwell.
McGrath, I. (2002). *Materials evaluation and design for language teaching*. Edinburgh: Edinburgh University Press.
Schneider, E. W. (2011). *English around the world, an introduction*. Cambridge: Cambridge University Press.

Smallwood, I., Li, P.-L., & Jin, L. (2004, 2005). *College English creative communication* (Books 1, 2, 3, 4). Shanghai: Macmillan/Shanghai Foreign Language Education Press.
Smallwood, I., Li, P.-L., Martin, S., & Green, C. (2002). *College English creative reading* (Books 1, 2, 3, 4). Shanghai: Macmillan/Shanghai Foreign Language Education Press.
Ting-Toomey, S. (1999). *Communicating across cultures.* New York, NY: The Guilford Press.
Tomlinson, B. (Ed.). (1998). *Materials development in language teaching.* Cambridge: Cambridge University Press.
Tomlinson, B. (Ed.). (2003). *Developing materials for language teaching.* London: Continuum.
Tomlinson, B. (2008). *English language teaching materials.* London: Continuum.

Martin Cortazzi
Centre for Applied Linguistics
University of Warwick
Coventry, UK

Lixian Jin
School of English, Faculty of Humanities and Social Sciences
University of Nottingham
Ningbo, China

LILIA SAVOVA

7. CONVERSATION ANALYSIS CRITERIA FOR EVALUATING THE AUTHENTICITY OF ESL TEXTBOOK CONVERSATIONS

INTRODUCTION

One of the most difficult and elusive ESL subjects taught seems to be conversation. Teachers have complained of having little success despite the effort involved, of feeling uncertain of what they are doing and why. Students have found conversation classes lacking in the kinds of conversations they see in life, in films, and on YouTube. ESOL specialists have described textbook conversations as stilted and inauthentic (Richards & Rogers, 2001), written in teacherese, even absurd (Ionesco, 1950). Thus, the ineffectiveness of textbook conversations and conversation classes has been linked to their lack of authenticity and to the lack of reliable principles of evaluating such authenticity. Furthermore, inauthentic conversation practices have been associated with poor ESL communication skills at all proficiency levels. With the advance of technology, publishers have been able to supplement printed dialogues with audio/video/online recordings of these conversations as well as use corpora to select authentic interactions (Richards, Hull, & Proctor, 2005). Yet, a sense of the fundamental artificiality of ESL textbook and classroom conversations persists.

To unravel this mystery, I will analyze sample textbook conversations in terms of what they actually do while claiming the development of conversation skills. I will demonstrate how in addition to linguistic analyses, Conversation Analysis (CA) could provide conversation criteria to evaluate the authenticity of textbook conversations. I will do so by introducing CA as a tool that helps illuminate the unique structural features of real-life conversations as well as apply CA in the analysis of a sample ESL textbook conversation. Finally, I will offer some criteria for evaluating the authenticity of textbook conversations, and, based on these, I will make practical suggestions for curriculum and conversations design transformations that might reverse years of misguided conversation goals and practices.

EVALUATING ESL CONVERSATIONS AS A TOOL FOR DEVELOPING LINGUISTIC COMPETENCE

Traditionally, textbooks have included conversations/dialogues to develop linguistic competence, or more specifically, as a way of practicing vocabulary and grammar.

Hence, the main criterion for developing and evaluating textbook conversations has been their lexico-grammatical content or the target vocabulary and structures. This approach follows from the assumption that language is a set of structures whose acquisition automatically leads to developing speaking skills, which are equated with conversation skills. For example, in the following dialogue, the participants are using the conversation format to practice vocabulary and grammar:

(01) A: Is your mother a nurse?
(02) B: No, she isn't. Is your mother a nurse?
(03) A: No, she isn't. She is a teacher.
(04) B: Is she an English teacher?
(05) A: No, she isn't. My uncle is an English teacher.

(Retrieved from http://eg21.co.kr/f_phone/file/general/Beginner01/Occupation.pdf)

The dialogue between A & B expects learners to practice vocabulary (e.g., names of professions) and third person questions, answers and statements with "to be" (e.g., "Is X a teacher?" "Yes, she is", No, she isn't". Y is an English teacher".). The sole purpose of this conversation is lexico-grammatical correctness. By that criterion, it seems fine. However, such an evaluation misses the point of communication itself. Pragmatically speaking, and, unlike real-life conversations, these language exchanges are entirely devoid of context. The interlocutors A & B are nameless. Their relationship is unknown. It is not clear who they are, where they are, or why they are having this conversation. One could hardly imagine this or even a similar conversation occurring in any conceivable situation, in any country or language. Thus, using grammatical correctness as the main criterion for evaluating textbook conversations could explain why foreign language textbooks, especially conversation dialogues, are sometimes compared to the theatre of the absurd.

Compare this to an excerpt from Samuel Becket's *Waiting for Godot:*

Pozzo: What was I saying?
Vladimir: Let's go.
Estragon: But take the weight off your feet, I implore you. You'll catch your death.
Pozzo: True. (*He sits down. To Estragon.*) What is your name?
Estragon: Adam.
Pozzo: (*who hasn't listened*) Ah yes! The night. (*He raises his head.*) But be a little more attentive, for pity's sake, otherwise we'll never get anywhere.

(Retrieved from http://www.shmoop.com/waiting-for-godot/religion-quotes.html)

Here, too, even though the characters have names, they don't seem to know their names. Well into the conversation, Pozzo asks Estragon about his name.

The latter then calls himself "Adam". Visibly, they seem to be talking to each other, or conversing. However, that is hardly the case. It is not at all clear who they are, where they are, or why they are talking at all since they are not exactly listening to each other or responding to what has been said before. While this existentialist play purposefully depicts human absurdity and alienation, ESL textbook dialogues do so unintentionally. By offering similarly meaningless language practice, they engage students in "conversations" that do not feel like conversations, do not look like conversations, and along with the simplicity of the language used, create a sense of being and sounding inadequate, especially among beginning adolescent learners who are in the process of building their adult identities.

In both examples, there doesn't appear to be a good reason for any of the interactions taking place. Thus, there is no clear answer to questions like, "Why is A asking B "Is your mother a nurse?" In fact, the questions and answers in these two dialogues do not make sense in terms of communicative functions, or language use. Grammatically, they are correct. But pragmatically, they are very far from being acceptable as real-life conversations. Such conversations illustrate the problems of relying entirely on grammatical principles for evaluating textbook conversations. They reveal the need for greater authenticity of ESL conversation practices and the need for pragmatic criteria for evaluating the authenticity of ESL textbook conversations.

EVALUATING ESL CONVERSATIONS AS A TOOL FOR DEVELOPING PRAGMATIC COMPETENCE

Beyond developing linguistic competence and in response to an increased interest in the use of language in society, ESL textbook dialogues have added some pragmatic features such as speech events (e.g., shopping trips, holiday scenes, travel events, school events, parties, etc.) and communicative functions or speech acts (e.g., asking for or giving information; making and responding to invitations; making, accepting and refusing offers; introducing oneself and others; etc.). These have been added as a way to bring conversation practice closer to real-life conversations. Applying these and other pragmatic criteria for developing and evaluating textbook conversations is based on the assumption that language is a means of communication and language learning is facilitated by a communicative or situational approach. However, the above communicative functions still focus on the target vocabulary and grammar items as their language exponents. Thus, little or no attention is paid to criteria for developing and evaluating uniquely conversation skills that are not related to vocabulary or grammar. For example, the following dialogue includes a speech event (e.g., ordering a meal) with several communicative functions or speech acts incorporated in it (e.g., introductions, requests, thanks, greetings) but still falls short of achieving conversation authenticity.

L. SAVOVA

At a Restaurant

Ordering a Meal

(01) A: Hi. How are you doing this afternoon?
(02) B: Fine, thank you. Can I see the menu, please?
(03) A: Certainly, here you are.
(04) B: Thank you. What's today's special?
(05) A: Grilled chicken and chicken fried rice.
(06) B: That sounds good. I'll have that.
(07) A: Would you like something to drink?
(08) B: Yes, I'd like a coke.
(09) A: Thank you. (Returning with the food) Here you are. Enjoy your meal!
(10) B: Thank you.
(11) A: Can I get you anything else?
(12) B: No thanks. I'd like the bill, please.
(13) A: That'll be SR 15.50.
(14) B: Here you are. Keep the change!
(15) A: Thank you. Have a good day!
(16) B: Bye.

(Retrieved from http://faculty.ksu.edu.sa/sajidchaudhry/Learning%20Resources/Dialogue%20at%20a%20restaurant.pdf)

At first glance, this seems an improvement. It is a typical waiter-customer dialogue where anonymity is expected and conversations are structured. However, from a CA perspective, there is a lot that is debatable. First, the opening (01) is a bit odd – waiters usually begin by introducing themselves, "Good afternoon. I'm Cindy. I'll be your waiter today". The customer's response to this opening "Can I see the menu, please?" might suggest that the waiter isn't doing his/her job well. Customers do not usually have to ask for the menu. It is offered to them even before the greeting. Furthermore, it's the waiter who recites the day's specials and not the diner who has to ask about them. The answer "grilled chicken and chicken fried rice" is quite puzzling: "chicken fried rice" is not a common menu item. Fried rice is but it is not a "special" by any means. The waiter's question, "Would you like something to drink?" is again quite inauthentic. The usual question would be, "What would you like to drink?" Towards the end of the meal, the waiter again asks an inappropriate question, "Can I get you anything else?" Usually, such a question is asked when the order is made. At the end of the meal, the waiter may offer the dessert menu and ask about that.

Thus, even though this appears to be a common speech event (e.g., "At a Restaurant"), its authenticity is compromised in several ways. First, the event itself is interrupted: we hear the waiter and the customer at the beginning and at the end of the meal, the "hi" and the "bye". What happens in-between is not there. Second, the language exponents used for the different speech acts (e.g., greeting, asking for and giving information, etc.) are grammatically correct but pragmatically problematic, so much so that quite unintentionally, the waiter's language use borders on impoliteness and incompetence. Last but not least, from a CA perspective, basic structures such as turn-construction units are of the simple Q & A type where each turn is assigned (Wong & Waring, 2010), sequencing practices are limited to generic adjacency pairs (e.g., two turns produced by two speakers and ordered as first-pair part (FPP) and second-pair part (SPP)) (Wong & Waring, 2010), while overall structuring practices, such as conversation openings and closings for waiter-customer conversations at the restaurant do not follow typical anchor points and topics at the beginning or at the end (Wong & Waring, 2010). Indeed, the waiter's closing phrase "Have a good day" without "Please come again" or anything similar to that may even sound hostile.

EVALUATING ESL TEXTBOOK CONVERSATIONS AS A TOOL FOR COMBINING LINGUISTIC AND PRAGMATIC COMPETENCE

So far, I have analyzed conversations retrieved from online sources, which may not have gone through the process of rigorous review. Despite that, they are fairly representative of both published and unpublished ESL conversation practices. Below, I will use a sample conversation from an ESL textbook (Richards et al., 2005) to illustrate how teachers using commercially published ESL textbooks could use both linguistic and pragmatic criteria to adapt and transform such conversations from traditional vocabulary-grammar drills and from "sentences spoken" (Sacks, Schegloff, & Jefferson, 1974) into pragmatically authentic conversation learning. In other words, I will demonstrate how using pragmatic criteria for evaluating and developing textbook conversations could improve the teaching of conversation as a subject on its own, and not just as a venue for vocabulary-grammar practice.

Unit 3. Unit topic: Could you do me a favor? Favors people dislike being asked. Conversation: Would you mind ...? [Richards et al., 2005, p. 16, modified]

(01) Rod: Hello.
(02) Jana: Hi, Rod. This is Jana.
(03) Rod: Oh, hi, Jana. What's up?
(04) Jana: I'm going to my best friend's wedding this weekend. I'd like to take some pictures for his Web site. Would you mind if I borrowed your new digital camera?
(05) Rod: Um, no. That's OK, I guess. I don't think I'll need it for anything.
(06) Jana: Thanks a million.
(07) Rod: Sure. Uh, have you used a digital camera before? It's sort of complicated.
(08) Jana: Uh-huh, sure, a couple of times. Would it be OK if I picked it up on Friday night?
(09) Rod: Yeah, I guess so.

The title and subtitle of this unit indicate that this telephone conversation will be about "favors people dislike being asked". The overt language exponents offered to the student include "could you ..." and "would you mind ...". However, what is expected is the completion of a speech act, which requires the mastery of a wide range of politeness strategies, an awareness of and sensitivity to a number of contextual factors (e.g., relationship between the interlocutors, time, place, reason for asking a favor, etc.), and the ability to select from a variety of language exponents, not just these two phrases, to achieve one's goal. The underlying assumption is that in English, asking for favors is to be avoided except on rare occasions from close friends and relatives. Thus, Rod and Jana must be close friends especially given the fact that this is an undesirable favor that will, furthermore, be asked over the phone. The latter is a challenging environment for such an arduous task due to the lack of facial/gesture feedback.

Using unique CA features (e.g., interactional, turn-taking, sequencing, repair and overall structuring practices, i.e., openings and closings) as criteria for evaluating the authenticity of textbook conversations leads to their enhanced pragmatic appropriateness. Thus, here, applying CA criteria to the analysis of this dialogue establishes an opening that is rather odd: The "hello" in (01) is a typical but also minimal way to answer the phone. Confirming that she is a close friend, Jana immediately recognizes Rod, even though his "hello" does not offer a self-identification. What follows, however, contradicts this initial impression. Given that Jana is a close friend, she doesn't need to introduce herself "This is Jana" (02). Furthermore, Rod's "Oh, hi, Jana. What's up" (03) continues the contradiction between close and distant: Rod's repeating her name makes her sound distant, while asking "what's up" treats her as a close friend. The opening statements (02) and (03) create the impression of distance rather than closeness. Working through such an awkward opening (e.g., summons-answer, identification-recognition, greeting, but no "how are you") (Wong & Waring, 2010), Jana abruptly arrives at the anchor point (04), where she raises the first topic (Schegloff, 1968), which is also the reason for the call. Such abruptness combined with her unwarranted expectations and presumptuous demand "Would you mind if I borrowed your new digital camera?" sounds a bit rude and even bullish. Such an impression is further reinforced by her dismissal of Ron's concerns "Have you used a digital camera before? It's sort of complicated" (07) with a callous and careless "... sure, a couple of times" (08). Ron's "That's OK, I guess" (05) and "Yeah, I guess so" (09) sound much more like a sign of resignation to harassment than an indication of willingness to do a favor.

The CA assessment of this dialogue has shown that pragmatically, it is a rather inappropriate, and possibly counterproductive example of asking for favors, especially difficult ones. It is inconsistent in representing the close relationship between the two interlocutors, and, quite unintentionally, suggests ways of asking for favors that might fail in real life.

Given that such pragmatically incongruous conversations may be common in ESOL textbooks, below, I will offer an illustration of how teachers and other ESOL professionals might be able to apply CA criteria to the evaluation, development and adaptation of textbook conversations and, thus, present students with pragmatically authentic models of conversations without changing the linguistic component.

(01) Rod: Hello.
(02) Jana: Hi, Rod.
(03) Rod: Hey, Jana, what's up?
(04) Jana: I'll be going to this wedding ...
(05) Rod: Oh, really? Anyone I know?
(06) Jana: Tim, our soccer coach. He asked me ...
(07) Rod: Tim, no way! That's amazing! Would that be Jessica?
(08) Jana: Yep. Um ... He asked me to take pictures at the wedding ...
(09) Rod: Wow! Are you sure you wanna do this?
(10) Jana: Oh, I don't know. I don't know why I promised ... because I don't have a camera.
(11) Rob: Mm ... That's interesting.
(12) Jana: Um ... Can I borrow yours?
(13) Rod: Are you sure? I just got it and I don't know how to use it myself.
(14) Jana: Well ... I know it's asking a lot ... but ... would you mind if I did?
(15) Rod: Ah well, what can I do. OK, I guess.
(16) Jana: Great! Thanks a million! Would it be OK to come and get it on Friday?
(17) Rod: Yeah. I guess so. I'll meet you at the Cafe at 5.
(18) Jana: That's perfect! See you then.
(19) Rod: See you. Bye now.
(20) Jana: Bye.

Here, I have applied CA criteria to evaluate and modify this conversation so that it represents consistently the close, friendly relationship between the interlocutors (01), (02), (03), (04) and their equal relationship where Jana does not just command a favor and Ron does not just oblige her demands. As an equal participant, Ron also interrupts (05), (07) to introduce his topic and to ask a question himself (07), (09), or to comment (13). Most importantly, I have applied CA evaluation criteria to demonstrate that to ask for an unlikely favor even from a friend, one needs to listen carefully, and not drop an inordinate demand like a bomb. Also, one needs to use language effectively to maneuver the conversation, drive towards one's goal but also prepare the other person for that gradually (04), (06), (08), (10), and quickly seize the right moment to utter one's request (12). Following a CA evaluation of the original conversation, I have also re-written it to represent all stages and discursive elements of telephone conversations (e.g., opening, identification-recognition, greeting, small talk with shared information, closing) leading to requests for difficult favors within a consistently informal register.

CONCLUSION

In conclusion, teachers could increase the authenticity of ESL textbook and other conversations by applying these linguistic and pragmatic criteria for assessing

Table 7.1. Criteria for evaluating ESL conversation authenticity

---

Evaluating linguistic authenticity

Situation authenticity: does the real-life situation used in the conversation allow for the authentic practice of the target vocabulary and structures?

Language authenticity: are the target vocabulary and structures introduced in authentic language exponents? Do people say such things in real life?

Evaluating pragmatic authenticity

Turn-taking practices authenticity: what turn-construction units (TCUs) are used to complete each communicative act? What lexical, phrasal, clausal, or sentential TCUs are used?

Basic sequencing practices authenticity: what generic sequencing practices (e.g., adjacency pairs, preference organization kinds, i.e., preferred vs. dispreferred), are used? What type-specific sequencing practices (e.g., agreement, disagreement, announcement, complaint, compliment response, invitation, request, response tokens) are used?

Topic-management and storytelling sequencing practices authenticity: what topic-management practices (e.g., topic initiation, topic pursuit, topic shift, topic termination) and story-telling practices (e.g., launching the story, telling the story) are used?

Overall structuring practices. Openings authenticity: what openings (e.g., anchor point, first topic, summons answer sequence, identification-recognition sequence, greeting sequence, how-are-you sequences) are used?

Overall structuring practices. Closings authenticity: what closings (e.g., mentionable "last topic", pre-closing sequence, terminal exchange, arrangement sequence, appreciation sequence, solicitude sequence, reason-for-the-call sequence, back-reference sequence, moral/lesson sequence) are used?

---

conversation authenticity and by asking these evaluative questions about the grammatical and pragmatic aspects of conversations (see Table 7.1).

The answers to these evaluative questions would prompt ways of writing or re-writing textbook conversations as authentic conversation experiences that are pragmatically appropriate and communicatively effective.

From a Conversation Analysis perspective, I have supplemented linguistic criteria with pragmatic criteria for assessing the authenticity of textbook conversations and for designing authentic conversations that use varied and complex turn-taking, sequencing, and overall structural patterns that adequately contextualize the target lexico-grammatical structures in a linguistically but also socio-culturally acceptable manner. I have also briefly summarized some of the basic linguistic and Conversation Analysis criteria for evaluating the authenticity of textbook conversations. Using these evaluation criteria, textbook conversations should not bear comparison to the theatre of the absurd of Irishman S. Beckett and Romanian E. Ionesco, whose *The Bald Soprano* literally reflects the non-sequiturs from his English textbook conversations.

REFERENCES

Beckett, S. (1953). *Waiting for godot.* Retrieved May 23, 2014, from http://www.shmoop.com/waiting-for-godot/religion-quotes.html

Ionesco, E. (1952). *The bald soprano.* Retrieved June 12, 2014, from http://www.pearltheatre.org/PDFs/SopranoGuide.pdf

Richards, J. C., Hull, J., & Proctor, S. (2005). *Interchange third edition student's book 3.* Cambridge: Cambridge University Press.

Richards, J. C., & Rodgers, T. S. (2001). *Approaches and methods in language teaching.* Cambridge: Cambridge University Press.

Sacks, H., Schegloff, E. A., & Jefferson, G. (1974). A simplest systematics for the organization of turn-taking for conversation. *Language, 50,* 696–735.

Schegloff, E. A. (1968). Sequencing in conversational openings. *American Anthropologist, 70*(6), 1075–1095.

Wong, J., & Waring, H. Z. (2010). *Conversation analysis and second language pedagogy: A guide for ESL/EFL teachers.* New York, NY: Routledge.

Lilia Savova
Indiana University of Pennsylvania
Indiana, Pennsylvania, USA

MARYAM AZARNOOSH, MAHBOOBEH KHOSROJERDI
AND MITRA ZERAATPISHE

8. EVALUATION OF ESP TEXTBOOKS

INTRODUCTION

English for Specific Purposes (ESP) is under the umbrella of teaching language for specific purposes (LSP) (Dudley-Evans & St. John, 1998). It is designed for a particular group of people with special needs in particular contexts (Hutchinson & Waters, 1987) and entails teaching language, discourse and relevant communication skills by incorporating topics and underlying methodology of the target discipline or profession (Dudley-Evans, 2001). ESP is mainly characterized by features such as being grounded on the results of needs analysis, drawing from topics, tasks, and activities of a specific purpose, and in cases benefiting from the methodology of subject areas or professions (Widdowson, 1983). Materials in ESP are related to the learners' special language learning needs. In fact, ESP is materials-driven and learner-centered and as a classroom-based program, concerned with practical outcomes (Dudley-Evans, 2001). Like any other program, ESP programs cannot be devoid of materials or coursebooks and the evaluation process to select textbooks and materials in ESP situations cannot be ignored.

This chapter reviews the main issues in ESP textbook evaluation which are well informed by the underpinned assumptions and principles of materials development. It briefly mentions the importance of textbook evaluation and the prominent status of needs analysis in designing and evaluating materials. This is followed by referring to the proposed language learning and teaching principles in developing coursebooks which need to underlie their evaluation. In addition, the prerequisite to any ESP textbook evaluation that is knowledge of ESP context and its specificity is discussed. Taking these aspects into account, the chapter ends with elaborations and examples of the two basic topics of evaluation criteria and methods without which no materials evaluation would be possible. It is worth mentioning that throughout this chapter, from time to time the term *materials* is used while the focus is specifically on textbooks as a type of material which is facilitative of language learning and can be informative, instructional, experiential, eliciting and exploratory (Tomlinson, 2012, 2016).

SIGNIFICANCE OF ESP TEXTBOOK SELECTION AND EVALUATION

Materials in many educational settings play a decisive role in exposing learners to the language specifically in foreign language contexts where the ESP classroom may be the only source of English (Dudley-Evans & St. John, 1998). Textbooks provide the basis of much of the language input and classroom practices learners receive and engage in. They also provide teachers with the source of instruction, content and structure of lessons, and balance of the skills to teach. Materials are considered to be essential within any curriculum and have more roles than facilitating learning. As curriculum models, they provide role models for classroom practices, and accomplish teacher development role (Nunan, 1998). Although textbooks are written to suit a large number of students in different teaching-learning contexts, no one book can be found to be perfect for a particular institution, a particular class or an individual in a class (McGrath, 2002).

The extensive literature on the necessity and importance of using textbooks and materials in ESP teaching situations carries the idea of evaluation with itself. According to Hutchinson and Waters (1987) evaluation is "a matching process, matching needs to available solutions" (p. 96). It is a systematic attempt to gather information and make judgments (Lynch, 1996; McGrath, 2002). It is "an intrinsic part of teaching and learning" (Rea-Dickins & Germaine, 1994, p. 4) and "fundamentally a subjective, rule-of-thumb activity" for which "no neat formula, grid, or system will ever provide a definitive yardstick" (Sheldon, 1988, p. 245), an idea also supported by other researchers in the field (e.g., Richards, 2001; Tomlinson, 2001, 2003c). Rea-Dickens and Germanie (1992) state that "there is a need to evaluate language teaching methods, materials, and their effectiveness as teachers and also how materials are presented to learners, the types of learning tasks used, and the way the courses are designed. They are all part of the curriculum taking place both prior to and during the implementation of a learning program, and they all must be evaluated" (p. 5). So the evaluation process should be carefully conducted to assure optimal results (McGrath, 2002).

While textbook evaluation or selection "signals an executive educational decision in which there is considerable professional, financial, and even political investment" (Sheldon, 1988, p. 238), textbooks may be evaluated for different reasons. Peterson (1998) states the following reasons: to make decisions on using textbooks or generating in-house materials; to select a textbook out of a number of coursebooks, and to examine a textbook in detail after choosing it to determine the areas that need to be supplemented. So evaluation is beneficial for selection of textbooks which is one of the important decisions to make in an ESP program.

ESP textbook evaluation is also important when both language learners and teachers are taken into account. It is important because numerous students around the world use available materials including textbooks to gain appropriate language knowledge to understand their disciplines and establish their careers and successfully communicate with members of their discourse community (Hyland, 2006). The process of materials evaluation also develops teachers' understanding and contributes to acquisition theories and pedagogical practices (Tomlinson, 2005). In fact, it helps teachers develop awareness by integrating their theoretical knowledge and their practice. It also helps them see materials as a fundamental part of the whole teaching/

learning process and establish priorities since one textbook may not meet all the learning/teaching requirements and needs which lead to decisions about the criteria that are more important to consider (Hutchinson, 1987). In other words, materials evaluation is important as it serves the immediate practical aim of selecting teaching materials and also plays a significant role in developing teachers' awareness of the assumptions of language learning based on which they teach.

NEEDS ANALYSIS IN ESP MATERIALS DEVELOPMENT AND EVALUATION

ESP as a language program aims to train students' subject-specific language use and develop their target competence based on their specific language learning goals. ESP courses intend to teach the language and communication skills that specific groups of language learners need or will need to function effectively in their study areas, professions or workplaces. To identify ESP students' goals, required specific language skills and to develop appropriate materials conducting needs analysis is crucial. According to Basturkmen (2006), needs analysis in ESP is a course development process in which the learners' present and target state of knowledge and skills, perceptions of their needs, practical possibilities and constraints of the teaching context are considered to determine and improve the content and method of the ESP course. Needs analysis not only plays a role in course design but also in "refining and evaluating ongoing ESP course" (Basturkmen, 2010, p. 19) through pre-course and ongoing needs analysis. Likewise, needs analysis is necessary and should be conducted for both developing and evaluating language learning materials and coursebooks (see Chapter 2 in this volume). Hyland (2006) also broadly defines needs analysis and states:

> *Needs analysis* refers to the techniques for collecting and assessing information relevant to course design: it is the means of establishing the *how* and *what* of a course. It is a continuous process, since we modify our teaching as we come to learn more about our students, and in this way it actually shades into *evaluation* – the means of establishing the effectiveness of a course. Needs is actually an umbrella term that embraces many aspects, incorporating learners' goals and backgrounds, their language proficiencies, their reasons for taking the course, their teaching and learning preferences, and the situations they will need to communicate in. Needs can involve what learners know, don't know or want to know, and can be collected and analyzed in a variety of ways. (pp. 73–74)

The needs analysis process includes the following aspects (Basturkmen, 2010):

- Target situation analysis: Identification of tasks, activities and skills learners are/will be using English for; what the learners should ideally know and be able to do.
- Discourse analysis: Descriptions of the language used in the above.
- Present situation analysis: Identification of what the learners do and do not know and can or cannot do in relation to the demands of the target situation.

- Learner factor analysis: Identification of learner factors such as their motivation, how they learn and their perceptions of their needs.
- Teaching context analysis: Identification of factors related to the environment in which the course will run. Consideration of what realistically the ESP course and teacher can offer (p. 19).

Needs analysis which was introduced through the ESP movement and considered as the cornerstone of ESP (Dudley-Evans & St. Jones, 1998) can serve a number of different purposes such as identifying the language skills learners need to perform a specific role (e.g., tour guide, sales manager, etc.), specifying if a course adequately meets the needs of potential learners, identifying particular learners' specific language needs, determining the gap between learners' present situation and target situation needs (Richards, 2001), and bridging the gap between insiders and outsiders' perspectives or assumptions (Widodo & Pusporini, 2010). While needs analysis serves as the basis of "informed curriculum practices, such as syllabus design, materials development, and instructional design" (p. 150), detailed or extensive needs analysis that precedes or accompanies materials and textbook evaluation may help teachers in making sound decisions about the suitability of ESP materials.

PRINCIPLES IN DEVELOPING AND EVALUATING MATERIALS

While needs analysis can serve as a basis for both materials development and evaluation, in the same vein, language teaching and learning principles may inform textbook design and evaluation. In other words, the principles and assumptions underlying materials development and the set of criteria proposed in this regard may contribute to a valid and reliable coursebook evaluation. Thus, textbook evaluation in general and ESP textbook evaluation in particular make sense to the extent that the principles that inform the development of such materials are taken into account when materials evaluation criteria are being set and evaluation instruments are developed. This is the issue we turn to now.

In his chapter on principles and procedures of materials development, Maley (2016) extensively reviews some principles, proposed by applied linguists and materials writers, which have much congruency and overlap and can provide the possibility of developing suitable materials based on sound grounds. For example, he refers to Ellis (2005) who proposes 10 principles of language teaching syllabus, Nation's (1993) 16 principles, and Tomlinson's (2011) principles of second language acquisition which are pertinent to the development of language teaching materials as listed below.

1. Materials should achieve impact.
2. Materials should help learners feel at ease.
3. Materials should help learners develop confidence.
4. What is being taught should be perceived as relevant and useful by learners.

5. Materials should require and facilitate learner self-investment.
6. Learners must be ready to acquire the points being taught.
7. Materials should expose learners to language in authentic use.
8. The learners' attention should be drawn to linguistic features of the input.
9. Materials should provide learners with opportunities to use the target language to achieve communicative purposes.
10. Materials should take into account that the positive effects of instruction are usually delayed.
11. Materials should take into account that learners differ in learning styles.
12. Materials should take into account that learners differ in affective attitudes.
13. Materials should permit a silent period at the beginning of instruction.
14. Materials should maximise learning potential by encouraging intellectual, aesthetic and emotional involvement which stimulates both right and left-brain activities.
15. Materials should not rely on too much controlled practice.
16. Materials should provide opportunities for outcome feedback (Maley, 2016, pp. 16–17).

Similarly, Hutchinson and Waters (1987) suggest six principles and four elements to consider in developing materials for ESP contexts which still leave room for teachers' creativity. Based on these principles, materials should stimulate learning, facilitate the teaching-learning process, reflect the perspectives on language and learning, mirror the nature of learning tasks, extend the basis of teacher training, and offer correct and appropriate language use models. The four elements they suggest include input, language focus, content focus, and tasks. Input may be of different types, such as texts, dialogs, recordings, diagrams, based on the performed needs analysis, which provide the learners with the opportunity of using their knowledge and subject matter. Content focus refers to learners' specialist areas which should be utilized to promote meaningful communication in the activities. The third element, language focus, provides learners with the chance of learning how parts of the language work together. Finally, since language use is the ultimate goal of language learning, the designed materials should include communicative tasks which provide learners with enough practice in language skills and content subject matter.

Considering the characteristics of ESP materials and general elements which need to be included in an ESP course and the guiding approaches in this regard, Widodo and Pusporini, (2010) propose the following eight guiding principles in ESP materials development.

- Principle 1: Teaching materials should have a clear set of learning goals and objectives.
- Principle 2: Teaching materials should contain learning tasks, which allow for students' schemata or background knowledge or experience activation.

- Principle 3: Learning tasks in the materials should allow students to explore their specialized needs and interests.
- Principle 4: Learning tasks in the materials should enable students to develop their language skills for authentic communication and content competence.
- Principle 5: In the materials, learning tasks should integrate language skills emphasized.
- Principle 6: Learning tasks in the materials should be as authentic as possible.
- Principle 7: Teaching materials should have impact on learner language development.
- Principle 8: Teaching materials should inform what roles learners and teachers play in and out of the classroom (pp. 154–155).

These principles are basic theoretical frameworks for ESP materials development or materials design in other areas. However, experienced teachers may adopt other principles based on the requirements of their teaching and learning context and their academic background and experience. In fact, since no one book fits all situations, materials developers' practice should not be confined to specific sets of principles but tailored to unique situations and contexts. By the same token, evaluators need to consider principles relevant and specific to each learning context in evaluating ESP materials.

ESP TEACHING-LEARNING CONTEXT

While textbooks and materials can provide learning opportunities for language learners in various learning contexts, in an ESP context which prioritizes specific learners' needs, and is characterized by its authentic materials, goal-related orientation, and self-direction (Carter, 1983 cited in Gatehouse, 2001) teaching ESP encompasses the following characteristics according to Sifakis (2003):

- Knowledge and skill: In ESP context, learners acquire content or specialized knowledge and certain language skills (e.g., business English).
- Competence in English for General Purposes (EGP): Learners' EGP skills which include the four skills and sub-skills are focused on to facilitate ESP learning and syllabus designing.
- Vocational competence: It is related to the learners' ability to perform specific professional tasks in workplaces and essential to shape the syllabus.
- Subject specificity: learners' vocational and EGP competence with their ability in dealing with subject-specific information integrate to improve their class participation.
- Compulsory/voluntary nature of learning: This feature can affect the learners' motivation so the teachers' role in organizing the lessons is vital to help learners learn the language and properly function in workplaces or academic settings.
- Cultural characteristics: This feature boosts learners' sense of cultural identity and enhances their motivation in ESP contexts.

- Beliefs about language learning: At the outset, clarifying ESP learners' beliefs about language learning will raise their awareness about various aspects of the ESP context.

Nation and Macalister (2010) also consider a balanced range of learning opportunities which should be provided in a language course. The four major kinds of activity which approximately require equal time include meaning-focused input, meaning-focused output, language-focused learning, and fluency development.

Meaning-focused input: This would include authentic texts for reading and listening with interesting topics which are relevant to the learners' age and interests.

Meaning-focused output: This would include opportunities for learning through speaking and writing and using language to express real meanings. The conditions for meaning-focused input and output are the same and writing letters, assignments, or stories and poems, role-plays, simulations, oral presentations, etc. are examples of such activities.

Language-focused learning: This involves learners' deliberate focus on activities with particular language features such as parts of speech, collocations, grammar, intentional vocabulary learning, etc.

Fluency development: This refers to learners' becoming fluent with features already acquired, to achieve automatic proficiency in coping with input, and in generating output. It might include extensive reading activities, listening to stories, writing fluency activities, speed reading, etc.

In any ESP context, materials should be carefully selected to mirror learners' needs, the goals, and methods and values of teaching programs (Cunningsworth, 1995). Widodo (2016) identifies seven key elements of ESP materials which are "(1) authenticity, (2) topics/themes, (3) texts and contexts, (4) knowledge and language, (5) tasks or activities, (6) representations of participants and social practices, and (7) pedagogical prompts. These elements emphasize the totality of what constitutes ESP materials" (p. 280). In addition, ESP materials should stimulate learners' prior knowledge and experience. In fact, their world knowledge, general level of linguistic competence, knowledge of specific topics and registers, and communicative ability should be considered and also developed in ESP materials. This calls for ESP teachers' attention to the selection of simulated or real contexts, texts and situations from the learners' subject area which will naturally encompass students' language needs, and to the application of authentic texts and tasks they use in their specialism or vocation (Harding, 2007) which are also strongly advocated in ESP materials design (Basturkmen, 2010; Belcher, 2006). This reminds us the idea that ESP situations are different from one another and should be studied in their own terms. Specificity is observed in ESP social context, learning goals and objectives, selection of materials and activities, teaching methodologies (Cheng, 2011), and language genres (Hyland, 2011) which all need to be appropriate to learners' needs.

ESP TEXTBOOK EVALUATION CRITERIA

Much of the literature on materials development reveals various criteria to help teachers evaluate or select materials. In his state-of-the-art article on materials development, Tomlinson (2012) refers to evaluation instruments, schemes, checklists, and models proposed from 1970 onwards and briefly mentions their focus of evaluation (i.e., textbooks or teaching materials), and in some cases the number of components or categories they include (e.g., Breen & Candlin, 1987; Cunningsworth, 1984, 1995; Harmer, 1991, 1998; Sheldon, 1987, 1988; Skierso, 1991; Ur, 1996). Tomlinson mentions that many of those evaluation criteria are specific to a learning context and not generalizable or transferable to other contexts without extensive modifications; however, there are exceptions such as Cunningsworth (1995) and Byrd (2001) who respectively consider the target learners, and the fit between the textbook and the curriculum, as well as students and teachers importance in proposing evaluation criteria.

Hutchinson and Waters (1987) divide the evaluation process into four stages including defining criteria, subjective analysis, objective analysis, and matching. The first two stages occur at the course design stage. In deciding about the preferred criteria, various factors may be considered some of which are typically related to learners' goals, needs, learning styles, proficiency levels, others are related to language teaching methods, classroom contexts and processes, and the potential of materials in inducing motivation, variety and interest (Rubdy, 2003). In subjective analysis, course analysis in terms of materials requirements takes place; then in objective analysis, the subjective analysis of materials is evaluated, and finally the matching stage helps decide about the suitability of the materials.

There are different types of evaluating criteria, universal or local (Tomlinson, 2003c), general or specific (McGrath, 2002). As Tomlinson (2003c) differentiates between the two types of criteria, universal ones are based on principled beliefs on effective language learning and can be used to evaluate materials for all possible learners. However, local criteria which are generated from a profile are specific to the context in which the materials are going to be used. Similarly, McGrath (2002) considers general criteria as indispensable features of any good teaching-learning material while specific ones are context related. Accordingly, he proposes a book evaluation procedure including "materials analysis, first-glance evaluation, user feedback, evaluation using situation specific checklists and, finally, selection" (Tomlinson, 2012, p. 149).

In designing and evaluating ESP teaching materials, Bardi (2013) takes components of communicative competence (i.e., grammatical competence, discourse competence, sociolinguistic competence, and strategic competence) into account as they are basic competencies related to the four language skills and enhance the development of integrated skills. The criteria Bardi proposes to be applied in developing and evaluating an ESP textbook for a public administration course include:

1. Type of syllabus and identification of students' needs
2. Student participation in the learning process
3. Development of communication skills and strategies
4. Integrating meaning and form in the study of grammar
5. Types and range of learning tasks and activities
6. Authenticity of texts
7. Authenticity of tasks
8. Development of learning strategies (p. 9).

Moreover, Context, motivation, appropriateness, methodology, and language are categories used by Brunton (2009) to evaluate an ESP textbook for the tourism industry. In addition, practical concerns, skills, strategies, variety of tasks and activities, and layout are the features considered by Baleghizadeh and Rahimi (2011) in evaluating an ESP coursebook on sociology based on Sheldon's (1998) model of evaluation. Content, vocabulary and grammar, exercises and activities, attractiveness of text and context are also the criteria used in Azarnoosh and Ganji's (2014) study to evaluate a textbook on management. The list of examples goes on and shows the diversity of criteria and categories used by researchers in evaluating ESP books taught around the world.

While various lists of criteria are proposed to evaluate general and ESP textbooks and materials, it is important to consider manageable number of evaluation criteria and questions (Cunningsworth, 1995) as well as appropriate ones. Tomlinson and Masuhara (2004, p. 7) suggest five questions to evaluate materials evaluation criteria which include:

1. Is each question an evaluation question?
2. Does each question only ask one question?
3. Is each question answerable?
4. Is each question free of dogma?
5. Is each question reliable in the sense that other evaluators would interpret it in the same way?

However, investigating the literature reveals that most of the proposed criteria do not meet these conditions and are not applicable in other contexts (Tomlinson, 2012).

ESP TEXTBOOK EVALUATION METHODS

Among different methods of book evaluation, checklists and frameworks are discussed here. Checklists are the most widely used approach to textbook evaluation. Some examples of checklists are Tomlinson (2008), Litz (2005), McDonough and Shaw (2003), Byrd (2001), Harmer (2001), Littlejohn (1998), Ur (1996), Cunnigsworth (1995), and Sheldon (1988). Checklists provide the researchers with a list of criteria of successful learning-teaching materials based on which researchers can evaluate the quality of the materials.

One of the advantages of using checklists is to provide an economic and systematic way to ensure that all relevant items are considered for evaluation (Cunnigworth, 1995; McGrath, 2002). However, using the checklist approach has not been without disadvantages. For example, a criterion like "competence of the author" (Tucker, 1987, p. 358) or a limitation concerning what "desirable materials should look like" (Littlejohn, 1998, p. 181) present some serious problems in book evaluation. Other issues such as demanding much time and expertise, being too imprecise hence not answerable, being context specific and not generalizable, and being confusing and lacking validity are problematic aspects that Mukundan and Ahour (2010) pinpoint after reviewing 48 evaluation checklists from 1970 to 2008.

On using checklists and their advantage and disadvantage, Roberts (1996) specifies that

> it is easy to see that people unfamiliar with materials evaluation, but beginning to read up on the topic, may say to themselves: "Some of these checklists are outdated, but which of the others should I choose?". Demystification is urgently needed here, if nowhere else. The answer is, essentially, "none of them". ... it is unlikely that any two teaching/learning situations will correspond exactly. ... checklists in the literature should be regarded as illustrative and suggestive only, and never as decretory. While some of the criteria they embody may be relevant to one's own teaching/learning situation, perhaps their most valuable aspect is that they stimulate thought about the *system* of evaluation and the *modus operandi* to be adopted. (p. 381)

In addition to the proposed checklists for materials evaluation, a number of frameworks have been proposed. For example, McDonough and Shaw (2003) propose a framework for textbook evaluation including external and internal evaluation. The external evaluation involves a brief overview of whatever the writer believes about the book which is normally explicitly stated. The details include the intended audience and proficiency level, the context of use, presentation of materials, grading layout and methodology, visuals contained, culture, and supplementary materials and learning resources. The internal evaluation which is more detailed covers the skills to be developed and their presentation in the material, supporting audio and or video recording, authenticity of materials, suitability of materials for different learning styles, and individual, pair and group learning activities. McDonough and Shaw emphasize that usability, generalizability, adaptability and flexibility are the four main considerations when deciding on the suitability of materials.

Rubdy (2003) claims that a good evaluation framework contributes to matching flexibility, adaptability, and relevance of a textbook with language learners and their varying needs. She proposes a dynamic model of evaluation in which the three categories of psychological validity, pedagogical validity and process and content validity interact. These categories respectively include criteria to evaluate materials based on learners' needs, goals and educational requirements; teachers' abilities, skills, theories and beliefs; and textbook writers' educational philosophy and overall view of language and language learning.

Chan (2009) also proposes a holistic evaluative framework of a six-step model to evaluate business English based on research findings, pedagogical issues, and the discourse of the business English. The pedagogical concerns include evaluating business meetings based on needs analysis, teaching approaches for the language of meetings, spoken grammar and authenticity, and learner autonomy; and the discourse features of business meetings are based on research findings about "goal orientation, structure of meetings, language and strategies used in meetings, and cultural differences."

Another ESP evaluation framework (McCullagh, 2015) proposed for medical textbooks is based on principles of materials development and ESP. The framework is built upon Malay's (2003, cited in McCullagh) distinction of inputs, processes and outputs in materials development and consists of two parts: an outcome matrix and an evaluation grid. The outcome matrix specifying types and levels of outcomes is developed based on the results of the needs analysis and Miller's (1990 cited in McCullagh) pyramid of four outcome levels (i.e. knows, knows how, shows how, and does) assessing developmental stages of learners' knowledge and skills. The evaluation grid specifies three categories and eight criteria for evaluating the effectiveness of inputs and processes in ESP textbooks. These criteria include some criteria from Dudley-Evans and St. Johns (1998) and Hyland (2006) "to evaluate how well ESP materials fulfil roles for learners and teachers" (McCullagh, 2015, p. 28) and some of Tomlinson's (2003b) universal criteria.

After reviewing evaluation instruments of about 40 years, Mukundan and Ahour (2010) came to the conclusion that developing evaluation frameworks can be more beneficial than detailed and inflexible checklists in that they can include clear, concise and flexible criteria. Tomlinson (2003a) also states that in generating evaluation frameworks, flexibility should be one of the central considerations since its realization ensures that the target learners, materials, and specific learning context are appropriately associated. Mukundan and Ahour (2010) also advocate using a composite framework which includes the use of three instruments, checklists, reflective journals and concordance software (see Chapter 10, this volume). In fact, triangulation of methods and sources meant to utilize various instruments in incorporating qualitative and quantitative methods in collecting data from insiders and outsiders may lead to a more reliable and valid evaluation of ESP materials.

CONCLUSION

In this chapter, issues related to ESP textbook evaluation were discussed. Considering ESP learning and teaching context, the importance of using coursebooks in ESP teaching context as well as evaluating them were mentioned. A review on the significance of conducting needs analysis in both development and evaluation of ESP materials, and language learning principles which need to be observed were presented. In addition, some of the criteria and categories, and checklists and frameworks proposed by scholars and researchers to evaluate textbooks and materials were introduced. As Bardi (2013) argues "the two stages in the 'life' of a textbook need to inform each other in the sense that textbook evaluation should be underpinned by the writer's approach to textbook design" (p. 9).

In evaluating ESP textbooks, if priority is given to satisfying learners' needs, attending to appropriate principles besides considering characteristics of ESP courses and materials are part of the wider picture of setting evaluation criteria and going through the evaluation process. Through ongoing ESP textbook evaluation, the match between many aspects such as the students' needs, the goals of the course and the selected materials may be ensured. What seems to be more logical in ESP materials evaluation is going through the preliminary (before an ESP course begins), formative (while the course is ongoing), and summative (at the end of the course) evaluation (Robinson, 1991). In other words, evaluation may be carried out at three stages of pre-use, in-use, and post-use (Cunnigsworth, 1995; Ellis, 1997; McGrath, 2002) which presents a more comprehensive model of materials evaluation applied for different purposes. While the pre-use evaluation helps ESP teachers select appropriate materials, they are recommended to conduct retrospective evaluation rather than predictive evaluation to check the influence of the materials they used to make necessary modifications (Ellis, 2011; Tomlinson, 2003c).

Since there are plethora of varied criteria for evaluation of ESP textbooks which are reflections of the priorities and constraints of each learning-teaching context and for that reason not applicable in all situations, we hope ESP teachers and practitioners find the information reviewed in this chapter beneficial in providing them with insights on preparing appropriate criteria and flexible tools to evaluate ESP textbooks more objectively.

REFERENCES

Azarnoosh, M., & Ganji, M. (2014). ESP book evaluation: The case of management coursebook. *International Journal of Secondary Education, 2(*4), 61–65.

Baleghizadeh, S., & Rahimi, A. H. (2011). Evaluation of an ESP textbook for the students of sociology. *Journal of Language Teaching and Research, 2*(5), 1009–1014.

Bardi, M. (2013). Developing public managers' English language communication skills – proposal for a textbook design and evaluation model. *Administration and Public Management, 20,* 6–24.

Basturkmen, H. (2006). *Ideas and options in English for specific purposes.* Mahwah, NJ: Lawrence Erlbaum Associates.

Basturkmen, H. (2010). *Developing courses in English for specific purposes.* Basingstoke: Palgrave Macmillan.

Belcher, D. D. (2006). English for specific purposes: Teaching to perceived needs and imagined futures in worlds of works, study, and everyday life. *TESOL Quarterly, 40*(1), 134–156.

Breen, M., & Candlin, C. (1987). Which materials? A consumer's and designer's guide. In L. E. Sheldon (Ed.), *ELT textbooks and materials: Problems in evaluation and development, ELT documents 126* (pp. 13–28). London: Modern English Publications and the British Council.

Brunton, M. (2009). Evaluation of highly recommended: A textbook for the hotel and catering industry. *ESP World, 8*(1), 1–8.

Byrd, P. (2001). Textbooks: Evaluation and selection and analysis for implementation. In M. Celce-Murcia (Ed.), *Teaching English as a second or foreign language* (2nd ed., pp. 432–453). Boston, MA: Heinle & Heinle Publishers.

Chan, C. S. C. (2009). Forging a link between research and pedagogy: A holistic framework for evaluating business English materials. *English for Specific Purposes, 28*, 125–136.

Cheng, A. (2011). Language features as the pathways to genre: Students' attention to non-prototypical features and its implications. *Journal of Second Language Writing, 20*(1), 69–82.

Cunningsworth, A. (1984). *Evaluating and selecting EFL teaching material.* London: Heinemann.

Cunningsworth, A. (1995). *Choosing your coursebook.* London: Heinemann.

Dudley-Evans, T. (2001). English for specific purposes. In R. Carter & D. Nunan (Eds.), *The Cambridge guide to teaching English to speakers of other languages* (pp. 131–137). Cambridge: Cambridge University Press.

Dudley-Evans, T., & St. John, M. J. (1998). *Developments in English for specific purposes: A multi-disciplinary approach.* Cambridge: Cambridge University Press.

Ellis, R. (2011). Macro- and micro-evaluations of task-based teaching. In B. Tomlinson (Ed.), *Materials development in language teaching* (2nd ed., pp. 21–35). Cambridge: Cambridge University Press.

Gatehouse, K. (2001). Key issues in English for Specific Purposes (ESP) curriculum development. *The Internet TESL Journal, 7*(10). Retrieved from http://iteslj.org/Articles/Gatehouse-ESP.html

Harding, K. (2007). *English for specific purposes.* Oxford: Oxford University Press.

Harmer, J. (1991). *The practice of English language teaching.* Harlow: Longman.

Harmer, J. (1998). *How to teach English.* Harlow: Longman.

Harmer, J. (2001). *The practice of English language teaching* (3rd ed.). Edinburgh: Longman.

Hutchinson, T. (1987). What's underneath? An interactive view of materials evaluation. In L. Sheldon (Ed.), *ELT textbooks and materials: Problems in evaluation and development* (pp. 37–44). Oxford: Modern English Publications.

Hutchinson, T., & Waters, A. (1987). *English for specific purposes: A learning-centred approach.* Cambridge: Cambridge University Press.

Hyland, K. (2003). *Second language writing.* Cambridge: Cambridge University Press.

Hyland, K. (2006). *English for academic purposes: An advanced resource book.* London: Routledge.

Hyland, K. (2011). Disciplinary specificity: Discourse, context and ESP. In D. Belcher, A. M. Johns, & B. Paltridge (Eds.), *New directions in English for specific purposes research* (pp. 6–24). Ann Arbor, MI: University of Michigan Press.

Krashen, S. (1981). *Second language acquisition and second language learning.* Oxford: Pergamon Press.

Littlejohn, A. (1998). The analysis of language teaching materials: Inside the Trojan horse. In B. Tomlinson (Ed.), *Materials development in language teaching* (2nd ed., pp. 179–211). Cambridge: Cambridge University Press.

Litz, D. R. A. (2005). *Text book evaluation and ELT management: A South Korean case study.* Retrieved from http://www.asian-Efl-journal.com/Litz-thesis.pdf

Lynch, B. K. (1996). *Language program evaluation: Theory and practice.* Cambridge: Cambridge University Press.

Maley, A. (2016). Principles and procedures in materials development. In M. Azarnoosh, M. Zeraatpishe, A. Faravani, & H. R. Kargozari (Eds.), *Issues in materials development* (pp. 11–31). Rotterdam, The Netherlands: Sense Publishers.

McCullagh, M. (2015). *A framework for designing and evaluating ESP materials for English and communication skills in the doctor-patient interview* (Unpublished doctoral dissertation). University of Portsmouth, Portsmouth.

McDonough, J., & Shaw, C. (2003). *Materials and methods in ELT: A teachers' guide* (2nd ed.). Chichester: Wiley-Blackwell.

McGrath, I. (2002). *Materials evaluation and design for language teaching.* Edinburgh: Edinburgh University Press.

Mukundan, J., & Ahour, T. (2010). A review of textbook evaluation checklists across four decades (1970–2008). In B. Tomlinson & H. Masuhara (Eds.), *Research for materials development in*

language learning: Evidence for best practice (pp. 336–352). London: Continuum.
Nation, I. S. P., & Macalister, J. (2010). *Language curriculum design.* New York, NY: Routledge.
Nunan, D. (1988). *The learner-centered curriculum: A study in second language teaching* (4th ed.). Cambridge: Cambridge University Press.
O'Neill, R. O. (1990). Why use textbooks? In R. Rossner & R. Bolitho (Eds.), *Currents of change in English language teaching* (pp. 148–156). Oxford: Oxford University Press.
Peterson, J. A. (1998). *A demonstration of a textbook evaluation procedure* (Unpublished MA thesis). University of Reading, Reading.
Rea-Dickens, P., & Germaine, K. (1992). *Evaluation.* Oxford: Oxford University Press.
Richards, J. C. (2001). *Curriculum development in language education.* Cambridge: Cambridge University Press.
Roberts, J. T. (1996). Demystifying materials evaluation. *System, 24*(3), 375–389.
Rubdy, R. (2003). Selection of materials. In B. Tomlinson (Ed.), *Developing materials for language teaching* (pp. 37–57). London: Continuum.
Sheldon, L. E. (Ed.). (1987). *ELT textbooks and materials: Problems in evaluation and development, ELT documents 126.* London: Modern English Publications and the British Council.
Sheldon, L. E. (1988). Evaluating ELT textbooks and materials. *ELT Journal, 42*(4), 237–246.
Skierso, A. (1991). Textbook selection and evaluation. In M. Celce-Murcia (Ed.), *Teaching English as a second or foreign language* (pp. 432–453). Boston, MA: Heinle & Heinle Publishers.
Sifakis, N. C. (2003). Applying the adult education framework to ESP curriculum development: An integrative model. *English for Specific Purposes, 22,* 195–211.
Tomlinson, B. (2003a). Comments on part A. In B. Tomlinson (Ed.), *Developing materials for language teaching* (pp. 101–103). London: Continuum.
Tomlinson, B. (Ed.). (2003b). *Developing materials for language teaching.* London: Continuum.
Tomlinson, B. (2003c). Materials evaluation. In B. Tomlinson (Ed.), *Developing materials for language teaching* (pp. 15–36). London: Continuum.
Tomlinson, B. (2008). *English language teaching materials: A critical review.* London: Continuum.
Tomlinson, B. (2012). Materials development for language learning and teaching. *Language Teaching, 45*(2), 143–179.
Tomlinson, B. (2016). The importance of materials development for language learning. In M. Azarnoosh, M. Zeraatpishe, A. Faravani, & H. R. Kargozari (Eds.), *Issues in materials development* (pp. 1–11). Rotterdam, The Netherlands: Sense Publishers.
Tomlinson, B., & Masuhara, H. (2004). *Developing language course materials.* Singapore: RELC Portfolio Series.
Tucker, C. A. (1987). Evaluating beginning textbooks. *English Teaching Forum, 13,* 355–361.
Ur, P. (1996). *A course in language teaching: Practice and theory.* Cambridge: Cambridge University Press.
Widodo, H. P. (2006). A needs analysis project in ESP materials developmen: English education. *Journal of Language Teaching and Research, 6*(1). 16–29.
Widodo, H. P. (2016). Teaching English for specific purposes (ESP): English for vocational purposes (EVP). In W. A. Renandya & H. P. Widodo (Eds.), *English language teaching today: Linking theory and practice* (pp. 277–291). Basel: Springer.
Widodo, H. P., & Pusporini, R. (2010). Materials design: English for specific purposes (ESP). In H. P. Widodo & L. Savova (Eds.), *The Lincom guide to materials design in ELT* (pp. 147–160). Muenchen: LINCOM GmbH.
Widdowson, H. (1983). *Learning purpose and language use.* Oxford: Oxford University Press.

Maryam Azarnoosh
Islamic Azad University
Semnan Branch
Semnan, Iran

Mahboobeh Khosrojerdi
Islamic Azad University
Sabzevar Branch
Sabzevar, Iran

Mitra Zeraatpishe
Islamic Azad University
Mashhad Branch
Mashhad, Iran

HAMID REZA KARGOZARI, GOLNAZ PEYVANDI
AND AKRAM FARAVANI

9. E-TEXTBOOK EVALUATION CRITERIA REVISITED

INTRODUCTION

Textbooks are considered as the most prominent and ubiquitous part of education all over the world. However, the advent of the Internet, along with the emergence of multimedia technologies, is revolutionizing this aspect of education and is substituting printed textbooks with their electronic counterparts. In the very near future, electronic textbooks (e-textbook) will be the preferred choice of both teachers and students (Lee, Messom, & Yau, 2013). Electronic delivery mechanisms are changing the conventional format of textbooks and are disseminating digital contents around the globe (Murray & Perez, 2011). The textbook market is being revolutionized by the digital age. This circumstance is leading to easier availability of e-textbooks. E-textbooks have been available for two decades. Nowadays, you can have access to the electronic format of most popular textbooks (Murray & Perez, 2011). The sudden growth of interest in e-textbooks may also be due to the explosive rise of e-reader devices and e-book apps. Devices such as tablets, PCs, Apple's iPads, and smart phones have caused an upswing in the favor of e-textbooks.

To select the most appropriate e-textbooks, it is recommended to evaluate them to find their potential strengths and weaknesses. The present chapter aims to elaborate on definitions of e-books, their advantages, and criteria required for their evaluation.

E-TEXTBOOK EMRGENCE

Today there are many electronic libraries or bookstores which distribute electronic materials in the form of documents, texts and especially e-books. According to Cavanaugh (2002), the term e-book is usually applied as a general category descriptor for the three parts needed to use e-book. The hardware of an e-book, reader or e-book reader, has the shape of a portable reading device, a handheld computer or other personal digital assistants (PDA) on which the book files are stored. There would be a desktop or laptop computer that is running a software program which shows the 'book' on its screen. The reader software, which is often built into the operating system of many handheld computers, is a program which shows the book file on a personal computer (PC) or reading device, and provides navigation controls, annotation features and other display functions.

Pérez and Alamán (2002) state that e-books have been considered just as books in electronic format or virtual documents made of some parts which can be put together to constitute directly readable real documents. Moreover, e-books represent the opportunity to spread out, investigate and capitalize on new ways to interact with information.

DEFINITIONS OF E-BOOKS

Different definitions have been provided for e-books or e-textbooks. To some extent, most of these definitions propose that e-textbook is the electronic format of conventional or printed books or textbooks. For example, the online Oxford dictionary online (2010) defines an e-book as 'an electronic version of a printed book'. Murray and Perez (2011) state that the most common format of an e-book is a digitized form of a printed book. Moreover, Manley and Holley (2012) believe that the term e-book refers to different senses and it is the context of use that determines its meaning. However, Hawkins (2000) defines e-book as any kind of book that is available in electronic format via different methods of a downloadable e-book, a dedicated e-book reader and through a web-accessible e-book. Moreover, Magnik (2011) believes that any digitalized document available to readers via a portable storage medium is considered as an e-textbook. Crestain, Landoni, and Melucci (2005) state that an e-book is the integration of conventional printed book with the addition of some features which are provided electronically. By the same token, Lynch (2001) suggests three interpretations for e-textbooks. To his mind, e-book may refer to digital content, to e-book reading device or to computer software or computer applications.

ADVANTAGES OF E-TEXTBOOKS

Much has been documented on the usability of electronic materials and many educators believe that electronic text will be the future of print. Electronic books have some features which can attract publishers, libraries or especial users. As the history of e-book proposes, it is still unclear what types of books can be transformed into electronic form by keeping the same effectiveness of the paper-based counterpart.

Many researchers have tried to summarize advantages and merits of using e-books and e-textbooks. For example, Jesse (2014) summarizes the findings of the studies done by Abram (2010) and Blackwell (2010) and tries to list and explain some of these advantages. Mostly, the main advantages of using e-textbooks can be categorized as cognitive, affective, and social benefits. This section aims to elaborate on some of these benefits.

Anuradha and Usha (2006) assert that e-books are becoming more common because they have several advantages compared to classic books. E-books have multimedia information, full-text searching, reference linking, flexibility in searching, selection of different kinds of fonts, and portability. Its reading devices have adjustable backlighting which enable e-book users to read comfortably in any conditions.

Selthofer (2013) also interviewed e-book users on the advantages of e-books who mentioned that "they are searchable, adoptable, easily linked to other digital documents, transportable, easily accessible and durable" (p. 95). Most of the interviewees stated that "reading an e-book was something new to them. They preferred the interaction with the printed book and its visual appearance" (p. 95).

Moreover, Murray and Perez (2011) believe that cost is the primary incentive for the growth of e-textbook market. They report that the price of textbooks has increased annually in the new century. Moreover, Young (2010) claims that the cost of textbooks is higher than the cost of tuition in some universities. It means that students have to pay more to prepare their required textbooks than to pay for the university. This soar of textbook expenses can be reduced by substituting conventional textbooks by e-textbooks. Baumann (2010) claims that it is cheaper to produce e-textbooks than to produce hard copy textbooks. It is because the production of printed textbooks accompanies other expenses such as expenses of book stores, publishers, marketing and administrative costs.

Availability is considered as another advantage of using e-textbooks. Jesse (2014) believes that e-textbooks are instantly available for download. On the other hand, e-textbooks do not go out of print. Furthermore, e-textbooks provide reading anytime and anywhere. This feature leads to ubiquity of e-textbooks.

Marczak (2012) states that e-textbooks enable students to interact with the content via different routes. Lee et al. (2013) claim that e-textbooks incorporate multimedia contents such as video clips, games, animations, and texts that all of these features enhance students' interest and motivation for study. Davy (2007) believes that these qualifications aid students to journey the content in a non-linear method. This lets students use their preferred learning styles and fosters the individualization of learning process (Hatipoglu & Tosun, 2012).

Ergonomic concerns and health issues are regarded as other merits of using e-textbooks (Jesse, 2014). Lee et al. (2013) state that students do not have to carry heavy paper books anymore. On the other hand, e-readers help students to have access to thousands of textbooks with no weight.

All these advantages along with many other features of e-textbooks such as bookmarking, highlighting, note-taking, being green or saving the environment, and annotating have caused the prevalence of e-textbooks among teachers and students. This fact highlights the significance of e-textbook evaluation. On the other hand, educators and instructors find it essential to evaluate e-textbooks the same as printed textbooks to select the most appropriate ones. The subsequent sections will focus on textbook evaluation in general and e-textbook evaluation in particular.

TEXTBOOK EVALUATION

Hutchinson (1987, p. 41) defines evaluation as a "matter of judging the fitness of something for a particular purpose". Textbooks should be compatible with students' needs by focusing on their interests and abilities. They should also be in agreement with the teaching style of teachers (Grant, 1987). McDonough and Shaw (1993) claim that textbook evaluation would be an effective process in its own right because it gives the teachers the opportunity to find the principles of the materials and facilitates their developments in the field. Moreover, material evaluation plays a significant role in language teaching and learning by enabling teachers to provide their teaching abilities and developing awareness of their own teaching situations.

Evaluation is considered a process in which information is gathered to be used in making educational decisions (Genesee & Upshur, 1996). This process consists of three major components. The first component is collecting information based on the students' background, learning processes, and instructional factors. The second component is the expression of the information and examining it with desired goals, or other information that you need. The last component is the decision-making process about instruction, students, and textbooks.

Different researchers have proposed variety of criteria to evaluate language textbooks. For instance, Byrd (2001) considers content or explanation, examples, tasks or activities and presentation or format as the main criteria for language textbook evaluation. However, Cunningsworth (1995) deems corresponding to the learners' needs, reflecting the present and future of language, facilitating learning in various ways and having a clear role as support for learning as the main features for textbook evaluation. Ur (1996) states six criteria to evaluate textbooks including curriculum, graphic, tasks and topics, content, language, and skills.

Nonetheless, Nation and Macalister (2010) propose three criteria for evaluating textbooks including: (1) goal, content, and sequencing, (2) format and presentation, and (3) monitoring and assessment. For Littlejohn (1998), publication aspects of textbook such as its physical appearance and design aspects such as tasks and activities are major characteristics for textbook evaluation.

Many other researchers (e.g., Breen & Candlin, 1987; Cunningsworth, 1984; Harmer, 1991, 1998; Hutchinson & Waters, 1987; Sheldon, 1987, 1988; Skierso, 1991) have suggested different criteria for textbook evaluation in which factors such as learners' goals and needs, their learning styles and proficiency levels, teaching methods, classroom contexts, motivation, and interest are emphasized.

PREVIOUS STUDIES ON E-TEXTBOOK EVALUATION

The same as all conventional textbooks, e-textbooks also need to be evaluated. Landoni (2010) believes that not much attention has been paid to e-textbooks evaluation. Moreover, the quality of e-textbooks has not been studied enough. Landoni also claims that a few studies which tried to evaluate e-textbooks were done in isolation and were dependent on all previous studies.

There are some resources which explain how to design e-textbooks for teaching and learning goals. Previously some projects have focused on e-textbook evaluation which include The *EBONI* project (Wilson & Londoni, 2003), the *HyperTextBook* project, and the *Visual Book* project (Crestani et al., 2005). The *EBONI* and *HyperTextBook* projects considered the development of suggestions for the design of e-textbooks, and the *Visual Book* project focused on the visual aspects of the production of electronic books.

Landoni and Gibb (2000) mention the following three factors for e-textbook evaluation applied in different studies:

- *Sense of directness*: is the degree of feeling that changes on the screen as the result of the users' actions. In a system with a high sense of directness, users can focus on the task that is to be done without the cognitive overload of understanding system reactions.
- *Sense of engagement*: is the level of interest the system makes in the user.
- *Sense of text*: refers to the feeling a user may have concerned with the structural and semantic structure of the text that is being read.
- Wilson, Landoni, and Gibb (2002) presented a methodology for evaluation of e-textbooks which consists of four stages. These stages include: selection of materials, selection of actors, selection of tasks, and selection of evaluation techniques.
- *Selection of materials*: Texts can be chosen for evaluation according to three parameters: format/appearance, content and medium. Moreover, Wilson and Landoni (2003) consider three subcategories in selecting materials including hardware devices, e-book reader software, and web books.
- *Hardware devices*: Users can read e-books on electronic handheld devices, which copy the size and portability of paper books.
- *E-book reader software*: Some formats, such as Microsoft Reader and Adobe Acrobat E-book Reader make electronic texts easier to read by preserving the structure of the paper book and some of its visual features such as typefaces, color images and page layout.
- *Web books*: Electronic books are accessible via the Web in various forms.
- *Selection of actors*: Four possible actors can be identified as the participants, the evaluators, the task developers and the task assessors.
- *Selection of tasks*: Different task-types are suggested to gather quantitative feedback from participants about the materials:

  a. Scavenger hunts, which involve participants in hunting through the materials selected for evaluation in search of specific facts.
  b. Exams, which involve the participant reading a chapter or a chunk of text for a short period of time, learning as much as possible in preparation for a short exam.

Selection of evaluation techniques: According to Wilson and Landoni (2002), four procedures are proposed in EBONI project (2000), for getting qualitative feedback about the selected materials: Subjective Satisfaction Questionnaire, behavior observation, think-aloud and interview.

The only checklist suggested for the evaluation of EFL e-textbooks was proposed by Marczak (2013). Marczak suggests a predictive evaluation checklist. This checklist consists of three main sections each of which includes some questions to answer. These main sections include layout and design, content and functionalities, and device, format and distribution. Marczak also suggests that to verify the validity of this checklist, it should be subjected under while-use and post-use evaluation.

E-TEXTBOOK EVALUATION CRITERIA

Although having a good design has been considered as the main criterion to judge e-textbooks, some scholars have already referred to other evaluation criteria too. It would be very useful to have a set of fixed criteria regarding standards, procedures and measures for evaluation of e-books and especially e-textbooks. In sum, the main criteria proposed by different scholars for evaluating e-books are as follows:

Appearance

When the place of the book in the digital world is changing, it is a necessity to consider the role of appearance in the design of e-books in order that commercial publishing developments are informed from a design, as well as content and technology factors, and are delivered to the end-user in a form which enhances their usability (Wilson & Landoni, 2001).

Multimedia and Interactive Elements

According to EBONI guidelines, readers distinguish one of the main merits of presenting educational materials in the electronic medium as being the ability to use multimedia sections such as video and audio, and interactive elements in the form of experiments and quizzes, all of which provide a useful alternative to print publications. Having the elements such as these can increase reader's a "sense of engagement" with the book, increasing likeability and their ability to remember the information being conveyed.

Hypertext

As Wilson et al. (2002) put it:

> Cross-referencing between the pages of a book, between the main text and table of contents, index, footnotes, glossary or references, and between two or more books is considered an important property of the printed medium. Readers strongly value the ability to achieve these cross-referencing tasks

in an electronic environment. This can be difficult to achieve with the same simplicity and effectiveness as flicking through paper pages, but can be made more possible in an electronic book by adopting a strong structure and a clear and simple navigation system. (p. 17)

Layout and Paging

According to Chen (2003), not only does paging play a prominent role, but is also helpful in verification for text organization and citation. Wearden (cited in Chen, 2003) believes that users prefer landscape rather than portrait format on the television or computer screen.

Functionalities

Crestani, Landoni, and Melucci (2006) assert that paper books should be kept but they can be redesigned to fit the technological environment. New features such as search tools and hyperlinks can be added for searching, personalizing, studying, skimming, etc. the electronic book. Then they suggest including a table of contents, an index, a search tool, bookmarking features and hypertext to enhance navigation as guidelines to consider in designing effective e-books.

Moreover, Chen (2003) believes in the possibility of integrating electronic books with other online or offline books and reference materials. As a result, this "can offer different modes of reading, it is also much more portable, able to include much more content and more convenient than a paper book. However, there may well be a limit to the length of electronic books" (p. 10).

Accessibility

Most electronic books are applied in an offline mode. Users should download electronic books from e-network to e-readers or personal computers and then read the content. We can also access electronic books on the Net, although some software programs like browsers are needed (Chen, 2003).

Legibility

According to EBONI project (2002), fonts should be large enough to be read comfortably for a long time. In addition, readers could select a font style and size to suit their individual preferences, so that it would satisfy their needs whether their vision for reading is perfect or low. Possibility of choosing a color that contrasts sufficiently with the background is another point. Using sans-serif typefaces for small text and avoiding italics are also suggested.

Although these factors are considered among the criteria used for e-textbook evaluation, they do not suffice to have a comprehensive evaluation of e-textbooks.

Therefore, more studies are needed to propose new criteria compatible with modern versions of e-textbooks.

CONCLUSION

Cunningsworth (1995) believes that the increasing number of textbooks in the market makes the right choice among the available textbooks difficult. E-textbooks are not exceptional too. It means the ever increasing popularity of e-textbooks and their variety in the market cause the same problem. Since the entire design of EFL/ESL syllabus is around the selection of appropriate materials (Garinger, 2002; Harmer, 1991), a need for evaluation of EFL/ESL textbooks is felt. It seems that the evaluation of EFL/ESL e-textbooks is twofold. They should be evaluated not only based on their language contents but also based on their digital features. This integration calls for a comprehensive list of criteria to evaluate both aspects.

REFERENCES

Abram, S. (2010). Thinking about e-books. *MultiMedia & Internet at Schools, 17*(3), 18–19.
Anuradha, K. T., & Usha, H. S. (2006). Use of e-books in an academic and research environment. *Program: Electronic Library and Information Systems, 40*(1), 48–62.
Baumann, M. (2010). Ebooks: A new school of thought. *Information Today, 27*(5), 1–4.
Blackwell, C. (2010). Literature, literally at your fingertips! *La Prensa*. Retrieved from http://search.proquest.com/docview/748740519?accountid=12085
Breen, M., & Candlin, C. (1987). Which materials? A consumer's and designer's guide. In L. E. Sheldon (Ed.), *ELT textbooks and materials: Problems in evaluation and development, ELT documents 126* (pp. 13–28). London: Modern English Publications and the British Council.
Byrd, P. (2001). Textbooks: Evaluation and selection and analysis for implementation. In M. Celce-Murcia (Ed.), *Teaching English as a second or foreign language* (3rd ed.). Boston, MA: Heinle & Heinle Publishers.
Cavanaugh, T. (2002). Textbooks: Opportunities, innovations, distractions accommodation? *Teaching Exceptional Children, 35*(2), 56–61.
Chen, Y. N. (2003). Application and development of electronic books in an e-Gutenberg age. *Online Information Review, 27*(1), 8–16.
Crestani, F., Landoni, M., & Melucci, M. (2005). Appearance and functionality of electronic books. *International Journal on Digital Libraries, 6*(2), 192–209.
Cunningsworth, A. (1984). *Evaluating and selecting EFL teaching material*. London: Heinemann.
Cunningsworth, A. (1995). *Choosing your coursebook*. Oxford: Heinemann.
Davy, T. (2007). E-textbooks: Opportunities, innovations, distractions and dilemmas. *Serials, 20*(2), 98–102.
EBONI (Electronic Books ON-screen Interface) Project. (2000). Retrieved from http://eboni.cdlr.strath.ac.uk/
Garinger, D. (2002). Textbook selection for the ESL classroom. *Center for Applied Linguistics Digest*. Retrieved from http://www.cal.org/resources/Digest/0210garinger.html
Genesee, F., & Upshur, J. A. (1996). *Classroom-based evaluation in second language education*. Cambridge: Cambridge University Press.
Grant, N. (1987). *Making the most of your textbook*. London: Longman.
Harmer, J. (1991). *The practice of English language teaching*. Harlow: Longman.
Harmer, J. (1998). *How to teach English*. Harlow: Longman.
Hatipoglu, N., & Tosun, N. (2012). The design of renewable and interactive e-book template for e-learning

environments. *Online Journal of Communication and Media Technologies, 2*(3), 126–138.
Hawkins, D. T. (2000). Electronic books: A major publishing revolution. *Online, 24*(4), 14–28.
Hutchinson, T. (1987). What's underneath? An interactive view of materials evaluation. In L. Sheldon (Ed.), *ELT textbooks and materials: Problems in evaluation and development* (pp. 37–44). Oxford: Modern English Publications.
Hutchinson, T., & Waters, A. (1987). *English for specific purposes: A learning-centred approach.* Cambridge: Cambridge University Press.
Jesse, G. (2014). College student perceptions of e-textbooks and e-readers: New ways to learn? *Issues in Information Systems, 15*, 235–247.
Lee, H. J., Messom, C., & Yau, K. L. A. (2012). Can an electronic textbook be part of k-12 education? Challenges, technological solutions and open issues. *TOJET: The Turkish Online Journal of Educational Technology, 12*(1), 32–44.
Landoni, M. (2010, October 26–30). *Evaluating e-books* (pp. 43–46). Proceedings of the third workshop on Research advances in large digital book repositories and complementary media at Conference CIKM 2010, 19th ACM International Conference on Information and Knowledge Management, Toronto, Canada.
Landoni, M., & Gibb, F. (2000). The role of visual rhetoric in the design and production of electronic books: The visual book. *The Electronic Library, 18*(3), 190–201.
Littlejohn, A. (1998). The analysis of language teaching materials: Inside the Trojan horse. In B. Tomlinson (Ed.), *Materials development in language teaching* (pp. 190–216). Cambridge: Cambridge University Press.
Lynch, C. (2001). The battle to define the future of the book in the digital world. *First Monday, 6*(6). Retrieved from https://doi.org/10.5210/fm.v6i6.864
Magnik, J. (2001). Printing on electrons. In B. Cope & D. Kalantzis (Eds.), *Print and electronic text convergence* (pp. 125–144). Melbourne: Common Ground Publishing Ltd.
Manley, L., & Holley, R. P. (2012). History of the ebook: The changing face of books. *Technical Services Quarterly, 29*(4), 292–311.
Marczak, M. (2012). *Developing intercultural competence in the foreign language classroom with the use of information and communication technology* (Ph.D. dissertation). Warsaw University, Warsaw, Poland.
Marczak, M. (2013). Selecting an e-(text) book: Evaluation criteria. *Teaching English with Technology, 13*(1), 29–41.
McDonough, J., & Shaw, C. (1993). *Materials and methods in ELT: A teacher guide.* London: Blackwell.
Murray, M. C., & Pérez, J. (2011). E-textbooks are coming: Are we ready? *Issues in Informing Science and Information Technology, 8*, 49–60.
Nation, I. S. P., & Macalister, J. (2010). *Language curriculum design.* New York, NY & London: Routledge.
Oxford dictionary online. (2010). *Oxford University Press.* Retrieved from http://oxforddictionaries.com/view/entry/m_en_us1242960#m_en_us1242960
Pérez, R. C., & Alamán, X. (2002). Creating e-books in a distributed and collaborative way. *The Electronic Library, 20*(4), 288–295.
Selthofer, J. (2013). Design of e-books: Readers' expectations in a comparative perspective. *Libellarium: časopis za povijest pisane riječi, knjige i baštinskih ustanova, 6*(1–2), 91–97.
Sheldon, L. E. (Ed.). (1987). *ELT textbooks and materials: Problems in evaluation and development, ELT documents 126.* London: Modern English Publications and the British Council.
Sheldon, L. E. (1988). Evaluating ELT textbooks and materials. *ELT Journal, 42*(4), 237–246.
Skierso, A. (1991). Textbook selection and evaluation. In M. Celce-Murcia (Ed.), *Teaching English as a second or foreign language* (pp. 432–453). Boston, MA: Heinle & Heinle Publishers.
Ur, P. (1996). *A course in language teaching: Practice and theory.* Cambridge: Cambridge University Press.
Wilson, R., & Landoni, M. (2002). *EBONI: Electronic textbook design guidelines.* Bristol: JISC.

Wilson, R., & Landoni, M. (2003, March 9–12). *Evaluating the usability of portable electronic books.* Proceedings of the 18th Symposium on Applied Computing (SAC), Florida Institute of Technology, Melbourne, FL.

Wilson, R., Landoni, M., & Gibb, F. (2002). Guidelines for designing electronic books. In M. Agosti & C. Thanos (Eds.), *Research and advanced technology for digital libraries* (pp. 47–60). Berlin: Springer.

Young, J. R. (2010). To save students money, colleges may force a switch to E-textbooks. *Chronicle of Higher Education, 57*(1), 1–8.

Hamid Reza Kargozari
Tabaran Institute of Higher Education
Mashhad, Iran

Golnaz Peyvandi
Islamic Azad University
Semnan Branch
Semnan, Iran

Akram Faravani
Islamic Azad University
Mashhad Branch
Mashhad, Iran

JAYAKARAN MUKUNDAN, SEYED ALI REZVANI KALAJAHI
AND ABDOLVAHED ZARIFI

10. INSIGHTFUL GAINS FROM RESEARCH ON ELT MATERIALS EVALUATION

INTRODUCTION

Developments in materials evaluation have, in most instances, taken the usual path. Many in the past believed that materials evaluation like most types of evaluation was summative, never formative nor developmental. As such, in most cases, the only activity that evaluation involved teachers was book selection. This type of evaluation, which was commonly referred to as predictive evaluation was widespread especially in free markets where books from numerous publishers were offered to teachers. In situations like in the developing countries including Malaysia, teachers, however, never had any say in book selection simply because the books were state-sponsored and the selection was usually done by authorities such as the textbook development office.

When teachers did have a choice of what books to use, especially in universities, most people would think that they would have the help of the thousands of instruments developed for textbook evaluation. Unfortunately, this is usually not the case as the age-old ways of evaluating textbooks through 'impression' have been found to be the best way of evaluating books for selection as 'experience' is more practicable than assumptions of what criteria are best for evaluating a book.

When discussing the benefits of research on materials evaluation, it will be useful to view it from the following angles:

1. The main areas of research in ELT materials evaluation, and
2. The benefit and impact of ELT materials evaluation on language teaching and learning.

THE MAIN AREAS OF RESEARCH ON MATERIALS EVALUATION

The major focus in materials evaluation has always been on the development of instruments for textbook evaluation. Why has this been so? Our assumption is that this is the easiest to do. It is very easy to list a set of criteria and then present it to the user. What makes it 'easy' for the developer is his lack of awareness of the complexity of the task from developing to revising, to redeveloping, to tests on validity and reliability after the completion of the instrument. As a result of the non-empirical basis from which most of these instruments are developed and the ease with which these instruments are published, we are faced with a problem: What happens when instruments are produced for which there are very few users? This vicious cycle of over-supply and under-use of textbook evaluation instruments comes from understanding of many users that instruments developed by others are not good for their own 'local' needs. The other assumption is that many institutions take great pride in ownership and they would rather develop their own instruments. This resulted in many institutions developing their own instruments for evaluation, and many of these instruments were tested neither for validity nor for reliability.

> There would seem to be a point at which celebration of 'welcome diversity' (Bloor, Swales, & Williams, 1984, p. 4) especially in tertiary-level teacher training becomes a smug acceptance of entrenched confusion, rather than a positive basis on which to initiate methodological development and coherent change. Nowhere is this state of affairs clearer than in the uneven quality of evaluation tools given to the thousands of EFL/ESP teachers trained in the U.K. each year. (Sheldon, 1988, p. 240)

Another area of research that was common was the evaluation of materials. Most of this type of evaluation concerned the evaluation of textbooks/coursebooks or modules. Many of these evaluations were Master of Arts theses or the equivalent, or Doctor of Philosophy (PhD) dissertations. Many evaluated textbooks based on evaluation instruments published in journals and books while some were adaptations of instruments to suit local needs. The methodology used was mostly Mixed Methods with a balance mix of quantitative and qualitative methods of data collection and analysis.

Instrument Development – Some Lessons for the Future

The form and structure of the instruments that are available are quite predictable and easily identified. Mukundan and Ahour (2010) reviewed 48 checklists for materials evaluation in the period 1970–2007. They were either quantitative or qualitative or had influences from both. Some required evaluators to do preliminary or initial evaluation before going into in-depth evaluation (McGrath, 2002; McDonough & Shaw, 2003). Many of these instruments offer challenges to users some of which are:

1. The developers have often used "buzz" words of the era or period in which they were constructed hence many of the terms can be either confusing or unknown to the user. Some instruments which specifically address approaches or methodologies may not be applicable to present contexts; some outdated approaches or methodologies referred to in the instrument make it in most parts irrelevant to the user. Instruments which are developed in the 1970s for instance may put emphasis on "pattern practice" (Tucker, 1975) as the Audio-Lingual Method (ALM) was very popular then.

Table 10.1. Difficulty analysis of items in the SEC

		Evaluators			
Section	Item	E1	E2	E3	E4
A. Bibliographic Data	1	✓	✓	✓	✓
	2	✓	✓	✓	✓
	3	✓	✓	✓	✓
	4	✓	✓	✓	✓
	5	✓		✓	
B. Aims and Goals	1	✓	✓	✓	✓
	2	✓	✓	✓	✓
	3	✓	✓	✓	✓
	4	✓	✓	✓	✓
	5	✓		✓	
C. Subject Matter	1	✓	✓	✓	✓
	2	✓	✓	✓	✓
	3	✓	✓	✓	✓
	4	✓	✓	✓	✓
	5	✓	✓	✓	✓
	6	✓	✓	✓	✓
	7	✓	✓	✓	✓
	8	✓	✓	✓	✓
	9	✓	✓	✓	✓
D. Vocabulary and Structures Grammar	1	✓	D	D	D
	2	✓	D	D	D
	3	✓	D	D	D
	4	D	D	D	D
Vocabulary	1	D	D	D	D
	2	D	D	D	D
Vocabulary and Structures	1	✓	D	✓	D
	2	D	D	✓	D
	3	D	D	D	D
	4	D	D	D	D
	5	D	D	D	D
	6	D	D	D	D
	7	D	D	D	D
	8	D	D	D	D
	9	✓	✓	✓	✓
	10	✓	D	D	✓
	11	✓	✓	✓	✓
	12	✓	✓	✓	✓

(Continued)

Table 10.1. (Continued)

Section	Item	Evaluators			
		E1	E2	E3	E4
E. Exercises and Activities	1	✓	D	D	✓
	2	D	D	D	D
	3	D	✓	D	D
	4		✓	D	D
	5	✓	✓	✓	✓
	6	✓	✓	✓	✓
	7	✓	D	D	D
	8	✓	✓	✓	✓
	9	✓	✓	D	D
	10	✓	✓	✓	✓
	11	✓	D	D	D
	12	✓	✓	✓	✓
	13	✓	✓	✓	✓
F. Layout and Physical Makeup	1	✓	✓	✓	D
	2	✓	✓	✓	✓
	3	✓	✓	✓	✓
	4	✓	✓	✓	✓
	5	✓	✓	✓	✓
	6	✓	✓	✓	✓
	7	✓	✓	✓	✓
	8	✓	✓	✓	✓
	9	✓	✓	✓	✓

2. The difficulty analysis of items in the Skierso Evaluation Checklist (SEC) (Skierso, 1991) revealed that 3 sections (D, E and F) were considered by evaluators to be difficult (Mukundan, 2004). Section D (Vocabulary and Structures), for example, had 52 (72.22%) out of 72 responses listed as difficult. Analyses of this nature have revealed weakness in instrument development. We are now more aware of some of the problems teachers face when confronted with evaluation checklists which do not 'speak the language of teachers'. Table 10.1 shows data which reveal how even the most sophisticated of checklists may not be useful to teachers in ESL contexts like in Malaysia.

Evaluation of Teaching Materials

There have been evaluations done on teaching materials; modules, textbooks or coursebooks and multi-media software. In the past few years, there have been several PhD dissertations which have looked at the evaluation of coursebooks and reported their findings in journals (Alkhaldi, 2010). Because of the nature of the PhD program, several dissertations which focused on materials evaluation were based on evaluation instruments developed by the researcher which have to be rigorously tested for validity and reliability. This cannot be said of some of the instruments which appear in book chapters or in some lesser known journals which are less stringent on issues connected to reliability and validity.

One unique contribution of a disciplined way into materials evaluation was proposed by Littlejohn (2011) which was more sophisticated than other ways of evaluating textbooks in the past which were merely dependent on the development of instruments that resembled checklists. Littlejohn proposed 'analysis' as evaluation.

Later on, other researchers started questioning the over-dependence on the mono-instrument model for textbook evaluation which placed emphasis on the checklist. Mukundan (2004), for example, produced what was then considered the first multi-instrument model which, he believed, was a more efficient way of evaluating textbooks.

The Emergence of the Composite (Multi-Instrument) Framework for Textbook Evaluation

The composite framework (Mukundan, 2004) was one that had three instruments for use in textbook evaluation. The reason for the multi-instrument framework/model was that textbook evaluation was a complex exercise which needed sophisticated use of instruments. The new framework retained the checklist and included two additional instruments for greater flexibility and effectiveness. The two additional instruments were the concordance software and the teacher reflective journal. Figure 10.1 shows the interdependence of the three instruments within the composite framework.

The two additional instruments in the framework complemented the checklist. The checklist while commonly used had weaknesses. Mukundan (2004) discovered that these weaknesses in fact were serious. There were items in the checklist which were beyond the capabilities of the teacher to respond to. The vocabulary section of the evaluation checklist sometimes required the teacher to determine if the loading of vocabulary within chapters/units of the textbook was appropriate or balanced (something quite impossible to do especially since some textbooks have up to 15 chapters with about 40,000 running words the start to end). Then other items would expect the teacher to determine if repetition and recycling of words was efficiently done – again something quite impossible to do. All these inadequacies of the checklist however can be managed with the use of concordance software. Texts can be digitized and concordance software used to determine loading efficiency and repetition and recycling efficiency.

The checklist also has limitations which will not allow the teacher to determine if for example, activities and exercises in the book are good. The teacher log or reflective journal which is written at the end of a trial lesson can determine if the book is good or bad in terms of its performance in actual classroom learning-teaching situations.

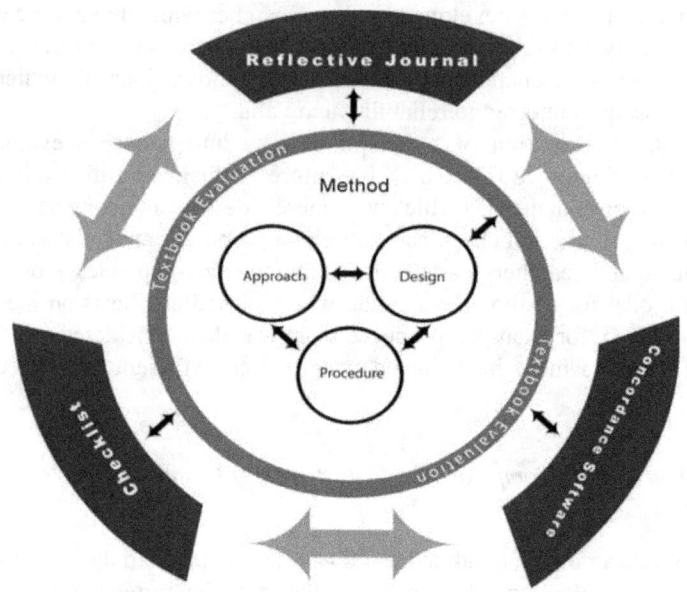

Figure 10.1. The composite framework for textbook evaluation (Mukundan, 2004)

The main advantage of the composite framework was that it allowed for the evaluators to have access to evaluation data from multiple sources and because of the use of three instruments then triangulation of data made the evaluation effective.

THE IMPACT OF RESEARCH ON ELT MATERIALS ON TEACHERS AND TEACHING-LEARNING SITUATIONS

The one basic belief that all researchers should have is that whatever research they undertake must not just be beneficial for the community of researchers but to the community of teachers as well. Research on ELT materials must be reported to teachers so that it not only informs them about the relevant and new knowledge in their career, but it may also transform them from passive materials users to dynamic ones. This would mean that researchers have informed teachers of new and more effective ways of developing and evaluating materials.

In the discussion that follows, we will provide an account of how research on ELT materials has benefitted the ELT community.

Research on the Textbook/Coursebook

If we view the way textbooks or coursebooks have been evaluated, the impression we get is that it is entirely predictive. This method of evaluation has negatively affected research on textbooks as it seems most researchers are conducting research on textbooks much the same way as evaluators go about selecting textbooks through predictive evaluation.

> My concern, then is with the analysis of materials 'as they are', with the content and ways of working which they propose, not, it must be stressed, with what may actually happen in classrooms. Analyzing materials, it must be recognized, is quite a different matter from analyzing 'materials-in-action'. Precisely, what happens in classrooms and what outcomes occur when materials are brought into use will depend upon numerous further factors, not least of which is the reinterpretation of materials, and tasks by both teachers and learners. (Littlejohn, 1998, p. 191)

While there are some researchers who have proposed 'analysis' as an alternative to conventional materials evaluation methods which use checklists, the fact remains that textbook evaluation is product-dependent and content analysis seems to be the main emphasis. The question we would ask is: What is materials evaluation good for if the book is not tested on its ability to engage learners in actual classroom settings? Investigations on textbooks should not solely deal with content analysis, rather there must be work on textbooks in-use, in actual classroom settings. Investigations such as these can help determine if the book contributes to learner-teacher engagement and makes lessons interesting, if the activities help achieve the determined goals, if learner motivation is sustained throughout the lesson or if the book helps with time management.

A lot has been written about what is perceived by researchers and practitioners as best practice in materials developed, some of which have been documented as 'principles' of materials development (Tomlinson, 2011); there, however, is not much to be said about the research that has supported these 'principles'.

One of the principles agreed upon by the ELT materials scholars is that concerning 'white space'. Tomlinson (2011) states that textbook pages should have "lots of white space" so that learners are not faced with anxiety and apprehension. A check on studies conducted on white space show that hardly anything has been done in the area. One M.Ed dissertation (Jin, 2010) investigated white space, comparing Malaysian locally produced textbooks (produced by local publishers with government funds) with those produced by established commercial publishers. The study confirmed the suspicion that local books lagged far behind those produced by foreign commercial publishers as limited white space was found in local books. The study assumed that the cramming in local books was the result of cost-saving measures which restricted the use of pages within the book.

One way in which we can determine if 'white space' matters in learning situations is to have intense classroom observations and to determine if learners are affected by the physical layout of pages and to what extent.

We do know that textbook writers write in an ad hoc manner, and this has been determined through analysis using concordance software. Two books (FB) and (SM) written for the same level by different publishers have shown that the books can have vast differences in physical outlook and content. Table 10.2 shows the extent to which the physical aspects of two Malaysian textbooks written for the same level differ drastically.

Table 10.2. Summary of the statistics of textbook 1 (FB) and textbook 2 (SM)

	Textbook 1 (FB)	Textbook 2 (SM)
No. of pages	203	219
No. of units	17	22
Ave. no. of pages per unit	12	10
Tokens	48,929	41,441
Types	3,856	3,678
Density ratio	0.1	0.1
Consistency ratio	12.7	11.3

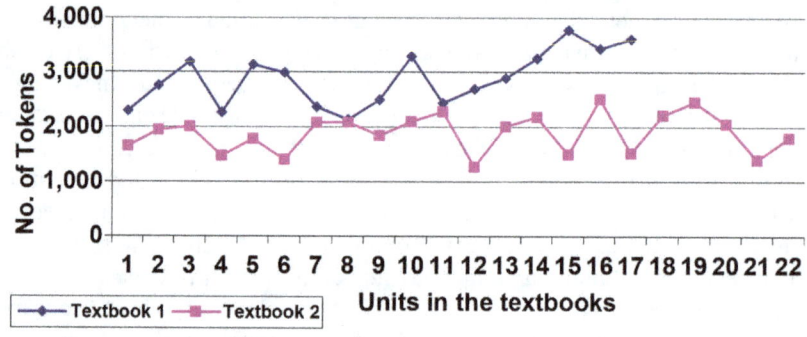

Figure 10.2. The total number of tokens in textbook 1 (FB) and textbook 2 (SM)

There are several assumptions one can make from these textbooks data:

1. Textbooks written for the same target group by different authors can vary vastly and this can have far reaching implications on learners and learning as the range of lexicon vary. This reflects on the ad hoc manner in which books are written.
2. Textbook 2 can be used for a longer period of time as compared to textbook 1; therefore, the teacher using Textbook 1 will probably be disadvantaged with less material for teaching.

Research of this nature should then get experts to overcome problems of this nature by intensifying and accelerating research in areas like wordlist creation. Wordlists created for levels of study will in some way help direct writers to which words are important to teach at which level.

Research on Learner Needs

Researchers have avoided the important issues that confront materials development, and some of those issues are associated to learner needs and relevance. The market has, however, continuously stressed that taboo topics like death and divorce are not permitted, but whose views are these, the learners' or policy makers'? It is widely assumed by most writers that textbooks should not include such issues which can invoke negative emotions in learners. But how can the theme of death be avoided if the language function 'to convey condolence' is to be introduced and taught to learners? It would seem trivial if one holds that it has to be left out of the textbook simply because it invokes negative emotions. Death is part of life and it, therefore, can be part of language readiness for learners. Perhaps, instead of removing the theme outright, policy makers need to probably allow writers to develop these themes using novel approaches that do not traumatize learners. Researchers should then provide many more alternative approaches to these themes which have been tested and the implications documented to provide guidelines to future writing on themes such as these. Researchers should then provide some alternative approaches for the presentation of these themes which have been tested and their implications documented in order to provide guidelines for future writing on themes such as these.

Research on Teacher Professional Development in ELT Materials

One area, which is neglected in the field of ELT materials, is research that helps teachers continuously develop professionally. Most teachers are developers and/or users of materials; yet, very few teachers rarely engage in evaluation of materials in retrospective manner, that is, evaluation of materials while in use. Retrospective evaluation of materials, which is usually done with the use of journals or logs, can help teachers decide on the parts of the book that need revision. Teacher professional development activity like this can lead teachers to become more expert on materials use and development. While Mukundan (2004) suggested the use of software for retrospective evaluation of textbook materials, the proto-type of the software, when tested, was found to be too demanding on teachers. It is then important for teachers to be aware of how important retrospective evaluation of textbooks would be in their professional lives.

CONCLUSION

There are emerging trends in research which show that conventional ways of researching teaching materials and evaluating them are beginning to gain momentum. Research on materials for classroom teaching-learning, for instance, has become more dynamic with the inclusion of learner needs, relevance and usefulness of the materials as important criteria. Trialing or field testing of materials then becomes so important that materials are viewed workable based on actual settings, not on notions of whether they will work or not.

The over-reliance on the textbook evaluation instrument widely referred to as the textbook evaluation checklist is also largely minimized a result of novel and more efficient ways. The emergence of the multi-instrument framework like the Composite Framework proposed by Mukundan (2004) shows the importance of triangulation of data in evaluation work.

There is still more work to do, and researchers should take into account the ways in which evaluation can benefit teaching and materials development and revision rather than merely account for materials selection. Thus, retrospective evaluation and the related investigations should have a larger focus than evaluation that is predictive and for selection purposes.

REFERENCES

Alkhaldi, A. A. (2010). Developing a principled framework for materials evaluation: Some considerations. *Advances in Language and Literary Studies, 1*(2), 281–298.

Donough, J. M., & Shaw, C. (2003). *Materials and methods in ELT: A teacher's guide* (2nd ed.). Malden, MA: Blacwell Publishing.

Jin, N. Y. (2010). Evaluating White space of a Malaysian secondary ELT textbook. *Advances in Language and Literary Studies, 1*(2), 220–232.

Littlejohn, A. (1998). The analysis of language teaching materials. In B. Tomlinson (Ed.), *Materials development in language teaching* (pp. 190–216). Cambridge: Cambridge University Press.

Littlejohn, A. (2011). The analysis of language teaching materials: Inside the Trojan horse. In B. Tomlinson (Ed.), *Materials development in language teaching* (2nd ed., pp. 179–211). Cambridge: Cambridge University Press.

McGrath, I. (2002). *Materials evaluation and design for language teaching.* Edinburgh: Edinburgh University Press.

Mukundan, J. (2004). *A composite framework for ESL textbook evaluation* (Unpublished doctoral dissertation). Universiti Putra Malaysia, Serdang.

Skierso, A. (1991). Textbook selection and evaluation. In M. Celce-Murcia (Ed.), *Teaching English as a second or foreign language* (pp. 432–453). Boston, MA: Heinle & Heinle Publishers.

Tomlinson, B. (Ed.). (2011). *Materials development in language teaching.* Cambridge: Cambridge University Press.

Tucker, C. A. (1975). Evaluating beginning textbooks. *English Teaching Forum, 13*(3), 355–361.

Jayakaran Mukundan
Faculty of Educational Studies
Universiti Putra Malaysia
Seri Kembangan, Malaysia

Seyed Ali Rezvani Kalajahi
School of Foreign Languages
Turkish-German University
Istanbul, Turkey

Abdolvahed Zarifi
Yasouj University
Yasouj, Iran

ABOUT THE CONTRIBUTORS

Saleh Al-Busaidi is an Associate Professor of English as a foreign language at the College of Education, Sultan Qaboos University, Oman. He served as the Director of the Language Centre at SQU (2010–2016). He currently teaches BEd and MA courses and supervises MA and PhD student theses. He received his BA in TEFL at Sultan Qaboos University in 1995, his MA in TEFL at the University of Exeter, UK in 1997, and his PhD in Curriculum Studies at the University of Illinois at Urbana-Champaign, USA in 2003. Dr Al-Busaidi has also participated in many national and international conferences and symposia. He has also published journal articles and book chapters on areas related to English language teaching and learning. His main research interests are: learner autonomy, curriculum and material development, study/academic skills, academic readiness and language acquisition.

Maryam Azarnoosh is an Assistant Professor of TEFL at Semnan Branch, Islamic Azad Univresity, Semnan, Iran. She was the Dean of Faculty of Humanities for two years and Head of Educated Women Council of Islamic Azad University Semnan Province from 2015–2018. She has also been the Head of Department of English language since 2010. She has over 18 years teaching experience and has published and presented papers in different national and international journals and conferences. She has also co-authored an ESP book for students of computer engineering and co-edited books on Issues in TEFL, entitled *Issues in Materials Development, Issues in Syllabus Design, and Issues in Applying SLA Theories toward Reflective and Effective Teaching*. Her main research interests include English language skills, materials development and evaluation, English for specific purposes, language teaching, testing and assessment.

Darío Luis Banegas holds a PhD in Applied Linguistics from Warwick University. He is a curriculum designer and teacher educator in English Language Teaching with the Ministry of Education of Chubut (Argentina). He mentors teacher research projects with the British Council and supervises MA and PhD theses with universities in Argentina, Colombia and Ecuador. His main interests are: initial teacher education, action research, CLIL, and materials development.

Martin Cortazzi is Visiting Professor of Applied Linguistics in the Centre for Applied Linguistics at the University of Warwick, UK. His strong interest in cultural aspects of language teaching, education and intercultural communication have been developed through extensive research, training teachers and teaching in China, Malaysia, Lebanon, Iran, Turkey, the UK and elsewhere. With Professor Lixian Jin, he co-edited three books (Palgrave Macmillan): *Researching Chinese Learners;*

ABOUT THE CONTRIBUTORS

Researching Cultures of Learning and *Researching Intercultural Learning*. Professor Cortazzi and Jin are series editors and authors for College English Creative Communication (Shanghai Foreign Language Education Press,) and authors of the Teacher's Books for the College English Real Communication series (Beijing Foreign Language Teaching and Research Press).

Akram Faravani is an Assistant Professor in Islamic Azad University, Mashhad Branch, Iran. She received her PhD in TEFL from Islamic Azad University of Tehran, Science and Research Branch. She has 10 years teaching experience and has published a number of articles in national and international journals and has presented papers in some conferences. Her major research interests include SLA, language testing, syllabus designing and materials development.

Lixian Jin is Chair Professor in Applied Linguistics and the Head of School of English at the University of Nottingham Ningbo China, after being Chair Professor in Linguistics and Intercultural Learning and having worked at De Montfort University UK for 23 years. She has taught linguistics, English language teaching, intercultural communication, qualitative research methods and clinical linguistics; and led collaborative research teams internationally. Collaborating with Professor Martin Cortazz and others, her over 100 publications focus on researching cultures of learning, intercultural communication, metaphor and narrative analysis and bilingual clinical assessments.

Hamid Reza Kargozari is an Assistant Professor at Tabaran Institute of Higher Education, Iran. His current research interests cover issues in psycholinguistics, materials development and sociolinguistics. He has been involved in a range of projects in these areas.

Mahboobeh Khosrojerdi is a faculty member at Islamic Azad University, Sabzevar Branch, Sabzevar, Iran. She is a PhD candidate at Islamic Azad University at present and a British council certified trainer and a TESOL holder. She is interested in holding TTC courses and workshops in teacher education. With 25 years of teaching experience, she has presented at ELT conferences and published papers and some books on ESP.

Thom Kiddle is Director at Norwich Institute for Language Education, where he has worked since 2011. He has previously worked in Chile, Portugal, the UK, Australia and Thailand in language teaching, teacher training and language assessment. He has a Master's degree in Language Testing from Lancaster University and the Cambridge Delta, and his role at NILE involves all aspects of academic management, and training and consultancy in a range of areas including testing and assessment, learning technologies, materials development and language teaching methodology. He is also academic director for all NILE Online courses and a former member of the editorial review board of the *English Language Teaching Journal*.

ABOUT THE CONTRIBUTORS

Jayakaran Mukundan is Professor at the Faculty of Educational Studies, UPM. He has won several awards for teaching, one of which is The National Award for Academic Excellence. He has also numerous research awards which include Gold Medals at the British Invention Show, London and IENA, Nuremberg, Germany. Most of these awards are for groundbreaking research in the area of ELT Materials. He has developed software for evaluating textbooks. Dr. Mukundan is keen on promoting professional development of teachers and initiated many international symposiums and conferences the notable ones being MICELT and ICELT. He also helped initiate the Regional Creative Writing Group which helps train teachers in the Asia-Pacific region to write and publish short stories and poems.

Vahid Nimehchisalem has been involved in English language teaching since 1994. He is a senior lecturer in the Faculty of Modern Languages and Communication, Universiti Putra Malaysia. His areas of research interest include self-assessment, assessing writing and English language teaching materials. He is chief editor of the *International Journal of Education and Literacy Studies*, an editorial team member of the *International Journal of Applied Linguistics and English Literature*, and is a regular reviewer of articles submitted to *Pertanika JSSH* and other journals.

Golnaz Peyvandi is currently a lecturer and academic member at Islamic Azad University, Semnan Branch, Iran. She is a PhD student of TEFL at IAU (Science and Research Branch). She has presented at some national and international conferences, is the author of some ESP books and scholarly articles. She is a reviewer of *Journal of Language and Translation*. Her major interests are syllabus design, CALL and comparative literature.

Seyed Ali Rezvani Kalajahi is post-doctoral fellow at the Faculty of Modern Languages and Communication, UPM, Malaysia. He obtained his PhD in Applied Linguistics from Universiti Putra Malaysia and his Master's degree is in English Language Teaching, Eastern Mediterranean University, Cyprus. He obtained his BA in English Translation Studies from Islamic Azad University, North Tehran, Iran. He has experienced teaching and conducting researches in different countries and his interests rely on corpus-based/informed studies, material development, and teacher education.

Carlos Rico-Troncoso holds a PhD in ELT at Leeds Beckett University, UK. He also holds an MA in Education and Social Development from CINDE and Universidad Pedagogica Nacional de Colombia. He works as a full time teacher at the Languages Department in Pontificia Universidad Javeriana, Bogotá. He has more than twenty years of experience as a teacher and researcher of Applied Linguistics in some universities in Bogota. Dr Rico-Troncoso has written articles and chapters about language methodology and evaluation, language materials and language competences.

ABOUT THE CONTRIBUTORS

Lilia Savova is Professor of TESOL and Linguistics at the Composition & TESOL graduate program at Indiana University of Pennsylvania. Her teaching and research are in second language teaching, assessment, instructional design, cross-cultural communication and linguistics. She has published many ESL books, book chapters, articles, and has presented at numerous international fora.

Abdolvahed Zarifi is an Assistant Professor at the English Language Department of Yasouj University, Yasouj, Iran. He started off his matriculation studies in 1985, and holds a PhD degree in ESL from Universiti Putra Malaysia (UPM). He is credited with being the first candidate who was awarded a pass with Distinction for his PhD Thesis in the history of the Faculty of Educational Studies, UPM. He developed a single-item test, Zar-Test, for the classification of different types of phrasal verbs. He also worked out the Focus Framework and the Cognitive Load Framework for the use and evaluation of vocabulary in ELT materials. His research areas of interest include ESL/EFL teaching, story schema, textbook analysis, corpus linguistics, etc. He is particularly interested in studying the English phrasal verb combinations.

Mitra Zeraatpishe is an Assistant Professor at Islamic Azad University, Mashhad Branch, Iran. She received her PhD in TEFL from Islamic Azad University, Tabriz branch. She has 10 years teaching experience and has published a number of articles in national and international journals and has presented papers in several conferences. Her recent works are three co-edited books, namely *Issues in Materials Development*, *Issues in Syllabus Design*, and *Issues in Applying SLA Theories toward Reflective and Effective Teaching*. She is currently working on another book in the same series: *Issues in SLA Research: Syllabus Design and Curriculum Development*. Her research interests include SLA, psycholinguistics, teaching methodologies, and teaching skills.

INDEX

A

Academic Word List, 6
Accessibility, 35, 36, 72, 117
Adapt, vii, 7, 8, 89
Adaptability, 104
Adaptivity, 33
Adopt, vii, 25–27, 100
Analysis, viii, ix, 5, 11–19, 21, 31–33, 61, 85–92, 95, 97–99, 102, 105, 122–125, 127
Animation, 113
Appearance, 113–116
Appropriateness, 18, 25, 90, 103
Assessment, 3, 6, 7, 11, 12, 23, 73, 74, 90, 114, 131, 132
Audio-lingual method (ALM), 122
Authenticity, ix, 3, 24, 32, 54, 67, 72, 81, 85–92, 101, 103–105
Authenticity of purpose, 24
Autonomy, 105
Awareness, viii, 2, 24, 27, 42, 43, 45, 46, 49, 50, 55, 56, 66, 70, 71, 73, 74, 79, 82, 90, 96, 97, 101, 114, 121
Awareness raising, 27, 79

B

Bilingual education, 23, 79
Book marking, 113, 117
British Council, 34

C

Checklist, 3–6, 11, 12, 14, 18, 102–105, 116, 122, 124, 125, 127, 130
Chunks, 15, 33
CLT, 23, 44, 49, 52–54
Cognitive development, 24, 27

Cognitive psychology, 48, 53
Commercial materials, 11
Communication, viii, 11, 14, 34, 43, 44, 46, 49, 51–54, 56, 65, 70, 71, 73, 75, 77, 78, 85–87, 95, 97, 99, 100, 103
Communication style, 68
Communicative approach, viii, 41, 43, 45
Communicative competence, viii, 41, 43–45, 47, 49, 52, 54, 55, 102
Communicative functions, 47, 87
Communicative interaction, 33
Communicative language competence, 46
Communicative language teaching, 31–38
Communicative needs, 33
Communicative tasks, 48, 50, 99
Competence, 37, 41, 43–47, 49, 54–56, 85–91, 100–102, 104
Complexity, 14, 33, 67, 121
Composite framework, ix, 2, 5, 6, 105, 125, 126, 130
Concordance, 5, 105, 125, 127
Conflict pedagogy, 48
Construct validity, 4
Contemporaneity, 32
Content, viii, 2, 11, 13, 14, 21–28, 34–36, 46, 66, 71, 72, 75, 76, 86, 96, 97, 99, 100, 103, 104, 112–118, 127, 128
Content and language integrated learning (CLIL), viii, 21–28
Content-driven CLIL, 23, 24
Content-specific, 24

Context, vii, viii, ix, 7, 15–17, 21, 22, 25, 28, 31, 35, 41, 43, 47, 50–55, 65, 66, 69–73, 75, 77–79, 81, 86, 95–106, 112, 114, 122, 124
Contextual reality, 32
Conversation analysis (CA), ix, 85–92
Conversation authenticity, 87, 92
Corpora, 85
Corrective feedback, 33, 36
Course analysis, 102
Coursebook, vii, viii, ix, 1, 21–28, 58, 65–82, 95–98, 103, 105, 122, 124, 126
Criteria, viii, ix, 3, 8, 11, 17, 18, 21, 32, 33, 50, 51, 65, 71, 73, 74, 78, 81, 85–92, 95, 97, 98, 102–106, 111–118, 121, 129
Cross-cultural pragmatics, 78
Cross-referencing, 116
Cultural authenticity, 67
Cultural beliefs, 43, 48, 65, 101
Cultural context, 43, 52, 53, 55, 66, 69–71, 73, 78, 81
Cultural frames, 68
Cultural identity, 55, 56, 100
Cultural knowledge, 56, 71
Cultural meanings, 41, 43
Cultural readers, 74–76
Cultural shock, 68, 79
Cultural values, 50, 79
Curriculum, vii, 2, 5, 7, 21, 23, 24, 26–28, 49, 51, 85, 96, 98, 102, 114

D

Data analysis, 16, 18
Denationalized, 67
Design, 7, 21, 47, 65, 66, 70, 72, 73, 75, 76, 79, 82, 85, 97, 98, 100–102, 106, 114–116, 118
Dialogs, 99

Difficulty analysis, 123, 124
Digital tools, viii, 31
Discourse, 27, 47, 77, 81, 95–97, 102, 105
Discourse analysis, 97
Discourse community, 96
Discourse competence, 47, 102
Diversity, 41, 45, 55, 67, 69, 71, 72, 81, 103, 122
Dual didactic, 49

E

E-book, ix, 111–113, 115–117
Economy, 4, 49
Electronic textbook (e-textbook), ix, 111–118
Empowerment, 21
Engagement, 8, 34, 56, 68, 71, 72, 75, 81, 115, 116, 127
English as a Foreign Language (EFL), vii, viii, 1, 11, 21, 23, 28, 65, 68, 69, 81, 116, 118, 122
English as a Second Language (ESL), vii, ix, 1, 68, 85, 92, 118, 124
English File series, 34
English for General Purposes (EGP), 100
English for Specific Purposes (ESP), ix, 95–106, 122, 131–133
English Language Teaching (ELT), viii, ix, 1–8, 21, 23, 25–27, 34, 38, 70, 74, 78, 81, 121–129
Environment analysis, 12
E-readers, 111
Ergonomic, 113
E-textbook, ix, 111–118
Ethnocentrism, 71
Evaluating criteria, 102
Evaluation, vii, viii, ix, 1–8, 11–19, 21, 22, 25, 28, 31–38, 41, 43–45, 53–56, 65–82, 86, 90–92, 95–106, 111–118, 121–130

INDEX

Evaluation criteria, viii, ix, 21, 65, 71, 81, 91, 92, 95, 98, 102, 103, 106, 111–118
Evaluation framework, 6, 32–34, 66, 104, 105
Evaluation instruments, 9, 98, 102, 105, 122, 125, 130
Evaluation methods, 103–105, 127
Evaluation process, 67, 78, 95, 96, 102, 106
Evaluation tools, 122
Experiential learning, 47, 48
Exploitability, 81
External evaluation, 104
EZText, 5

F
Face, 37, 56, 78
Feedback, 4, 5, 15, 33–37, 73, 78, 90, 99, 102, 115
Flexibility, 3, 24, 26, 50, 104, 105, 112, 125
FLT (foreign language teaching), 43, 55, 56, 74
Fluency, 3, 78, 101
Focus on form, 27, 33, 34, 36
Footnotes, 116
Foreign Language Teaching and Research Press, 74
Format, 5, 16, 26, 77, 86, 111, 112, 114–117
Formative evaluation, 6, 8, 106, 121
Functionalities, 116, 117

G
General competence, 45
Generalizability, 5, 104
General Service List, 6
Generic checklists, 12
Global English, 70
Goal, vii. 11, 13, 14, 16, 53, 85, 90, 91, 97, 99, 100–102, 104–106, 114, 123, 127

Graded readers, 32, 37
Grammar, 3, 23, 33, 44, 45, 54, 65. 85–87, 89, 101, 103, 105, 123
Grammatical competence, 102

H
HAMLET, 5
Hardware, 37, 111, 115
Higher-order thinking, 26, 27
Holistic judgments, 2
HyperResearch, 5
Hypertext, 116, 117

I
Immersion program, 23
Impressionistic evaluation, 2, 3
Inclusivity, 72, 81
Individualization, 113
Input, 16, 24, 27, 33, 36, 96, 99, 101, 105
Institutional needs, 21
Instrument, 4, 7, 8, 14, 16, 17, 41, 121, 122, 124, 125, 130
Integration, 49, 65, 72, 81, 82, 112, 118
Interaction, vii, 33, 35, 37, 42–44, 48, 50, 51, 53, 55, 56, 68, 73, 74, 78, 79, 85, 87, 113
Interactive whiteboards, 32, 33, 37
Intercultural approach, viii, 41
Intercultural awareness, 45, 79
Intercultural communication, 49, 65, 71, 75, 78, 80
Intercultural communication, 49, 65, 71, 75, 78, 80
Intercultural communicative competence (ICC), viii, 41–56
Intercultural context, 52, 71
Intercultural education, 48
Intercultural exchange, 41
Intercultural learning, 47–49, 71
Intercultural speaker, 43, 54
Internal evaluation, 104
Interviews, 15, 62, 63, 75, 115

137

Intra-cultural context, 52
In-use evaluation, 7
Investment, 18, 22, 33, 96, 99

J
Jing, 36

L
Lacks, 12
Language competence, 45, 46, 52, 56
Language diversity, 69
Language-driven CLIL, 23, 24
Language-focused learning, 101
Language for specific purposes (LSP), 95
Language use, 11, 43–45, 47, 52–54, 65, 68, 87, 89, 91, 97, 99
Layout, 3, 103, 104, 115–117, 124, 127
Learner factor analysis, 98
Learners' voices, 24
Learning aids, 31
Learning needs, 12, 95
Learning styles, 99, 102, 104, 113, 114
Legibility, 117–118
Lexico-grammatical content, 86
Linguistic analysis, ix, 85, 92
Linguistic anthropology, 68
Linguistic competence, 44, 46, 47, 85–87, 101
Linguistic varieties, 70
Literature, 3, 4, 11, 16, 21, 25, 65, 75, 77, 96, 102, 103, 104
Loading efficiency, 125
Local culture, 70
Local identity, 70
Local needs, 122
Lower-order thinking, 24, 26

M
Macmillan, 34, 74
Materials, vii, viii, ix, 1, 7, 8, 11–19, 21–26, 32–34, 37, 43, 51–53, 66–74, 77, 81, 95–106, 111, 112, 114–118, 121–130

Materials development, vii, 21, 32, 53, 95, 97–100, 102, 105, 127, 129, 130
Meaning-focused input, 101
Meaning-focused output, 101
Mediation, 23
Methodology, 3, 18, 32, 49, 52, 53, 95, 103, 104, 115, 122
Methods, ix, 2, 5, 8, 34, 95–97, 101–105, 112–115, 122, 126, 127
MicroConcrd, 5
Mixed methods, 122
Monitoring, 114
MonoConc Pro, 5
Motivation, 18, 26, 27, 46, 98, 100, 102, 103, 113, 114, 127
Multimedia, 111–113, 116, 124
Multimodality, 33

N
National context, 69
Necessities, 12
Needs, vii, viii, ix, 2–4, 6–8, 11–19, 21–28, 31, 33, 42, 47, 48–51, 55, 56, 65, 66, 68, 70, 78, 87, 89–91, 95–106, 113, 114, 117, 118, 122, 129
Needs analysis, viii, ix, 11–19, 31, 95, 97–99, 105
Needs assessment, 12
Non-verbal communication, 51
Note-taking, 113

O
Objective analysis, 102
Objective needs, 12
Objectives, vii, vii, 2, 3, 6–8, 12–14, 33, 36, 37, 51, 54, 58, 67, 99, 101, 102
Observation, 14, 15, 32, 33, 36, 115, 127
Orchestration, 33
Otherization, 67
Otherness, 56

Outcome, vii, 2–5, 7, 8, 11, 17, 32, 52, 53, 95, 99, 105, 127
Output, 33, 101, 105

P
Participation, 33, 34, 44, 78–81, 100, 103
Pedagogic validity, 71, 73, 81, 104
Performance, 17, 43, 44, 54, 77, 125
Personal digital assistant (PDA), 111
Personalization, 33
Phonemic chart, 34, 37
Physical resources, 32
Physical teaching aids, viii, 31, 35
Policy makers, 66, 129
Politeness, 47, 79, 90
Post-use evaluation, 7, 116
Practicality, 4, 14, 81
Pragmatic competence, 47, 87–91
Predictive evaluation, 6, 106, 116, 121, 127
Preliminary evaluation, 106, 122
Present situation analysis, 97
Present situation needs, 98
Presupposition, 66, 67
Pre-use evaluation, 6, 106
Process and content validity, 104
Professional development, ix, 22, 28, 71, 75, 129
Prognostic evaluation, 6
Program centered checklists, 11
Progressive evaluation, 6
Psychological validity, 104

Q
Qualitative checklists, 3, 122
Quantitative checklists, 3, 6, 122
Questionnaires, 15, 60, 115

R
Realia, 31
Real-life conversation, ix, 85, 87
Recycle, 4
Recycling, 27, 125

Reductionism, 67
Reflective logs, 4, 6
Reflective journal, 105, 125
Reflective thinking, 69
Reflexive principle, 69
Reflexivity, viii, 65, 67, 69, 71, 72, 75, 76, 80, 81
Reification, 67, 71
Relevance, 8, 13–15, 70, 72, 81, 104, 129
Reliability, 3, 4, 8, 14 16, 121, 122, 125
Representation, 21, 33–35, 37, 44, 53, 72, 74, 81, 101
Retrospective evaluation, 106, 129, 130
Retrotext-E, 5, 6
Rhetoric, 68

S
Savoir, 42, 43, 45, 46, 55, 56
Savoir-apprendre, 42, 46, 55
Savoir-comprendre, 42, 55
Savoir-être, 42, 46, 56
Savoir-faire, 42, 46, 55
Savoirs' engager, 42, 56
Scaffolding, 23
Scale-based evaluation, 3–4
Schemata, 47, 99
Schemes, 102
Screen-capture software, 36, 37
Selection, vii, 2, 11, 19, 32, 70, 72, 81, 96, 101, 102, 112, 115, 118, 121, 130
Sequencing, 27, 89, 90, 92, 114
Shanghai Foreign Language Education Press, 74
Shaping, 33
Situational analysis, 12, 87
SLA, vii, 32–35
Social awareness, 71
Social class, 68
Social commitment, 72
Social context, 43, 65, 69, 75, 79, 101
Social engagement, 68, 81

INDEX

Social identity, 56, 76
Social inclusivity, 72, 81
Social interaction, 51, 68, 79
Socio-cultural context, 70, 71
Socio-cultural diversity, 72
Socio-cultural features, 65–67, 72, 77
Socio-cultural information, 68
Socio-cultural knowledge, 45, 66
Socio-cultural orientation, viii, 67
Socio-cultural perspectives, viii, 65–82
Socio-cultural settings, 23,
Socio-cultural skills, 65, 69, 71, 73, 82
Sociolinguistic competence, 47, 102
Sociolinguistics, 47
Sociology, 103
Socio-moral legitimacy, 72, 81
Software packages, 2, 5
Source culture, 69
Specificity, ix, 95, 100, 101
Speech acts, 87, 89, 90
Speech events, 87, 88
Stabilization, 67
Stakeholders, 7, 8, 13–15
State board, 32
Stereotyping, 71
Strategic competence, 102
Structured reflective logs, 4–5
Student-led evaluation, 31
Stylistics, 23
Subjective analysis, 102
Subjective evaluation, 3, 8, 96, 102
Subjective needs, 12
Subjectivity, 3, 17, 22
Subject-specific, 27, 97, 100
Summative evaluation, 8, 106, 121
Supplementary materials, 37, 73, 104
Syllabus, 1, 2, 7, 37, 53, 72, 74, 103, 118
Syllabus design, vii, 1, 6, 7, 98, 100

T
Target culture, 53, 56, 65, 67, 69, 70
Target needs, 12
Target situation analysis, 97
Target situation needs, 98
Task, 2, 4, 7, 8, 11, 14–17, 23, 24, 28, 33, 34, 48–50, 52, 53, 72, 76–78, 81, 90, 95–97, 99–101, 103, 114–116, 121, 127
Task based learning (TBL), 23, 52
Teacher development, 67, 77, 81, 96
Teacher-led evaluation, 32
Teacher log, 2, 4–6, 125
Teaching aids, viii, 31–38
Teaching context analysis, 98
Teaching style, 114
Technical jargon, 4
TEFL, vii, viii, 65, 67, 69, 71, 73, 74, 77, 82
Textbook, vii, viii, ix, 1–3, 7, 11, 18, 32, 66, 69, 70, 85–92, 95–106, 111–118, 121, 122, 124–130
Text driven approach (TDA), 52, 53
TextQuest, 5
Themes, vii, 49, 51, 53, 73, 75–77, 81, 101, 129
Thinking skills, 23, 26, 27, 75
Top-down educational system, 6
Topic-based learning, 27
Topic-management, 92
Topics, vii, 1, 15, 26, 51, 73, 75–79, 81, 89, 95, 101, 114, 129
Triangular didactic, 49
Triangulation, 105, 126, 130
Turn-taking, 90, 92

U
Unidimensionality, 4
Uniformity, 67
Unstructured reflective logs, 4
Usability, 104, 112, 116

V
Validity, 3, 4, 8, 14, 71, 73, 81, 104, 116, 121, 122, 125
Veridicality, 72, 81
Video clips, 113

Vocabulary, 3–6, 24, 27, 54, 65, 77, 85–87, 89, 92, 101, 103, 123–125
Vocabulary distribution, 4, 5
Vocabulary load, 4, 5
Vocational competence, 100

W
Wants, 12, 21, 50
Web books, 115

White space, 127
WordNet, 5
WordSmith, 5, 6
World English, 70
World Englishes, 70, 77
Worthwhileness, 72, 82

Z
Zone of proximal development (ZPD), 36

www.ingramcontent.com/pod-product-compliance
Lightning Source LLC
Chambersburg PA
CBHW052129300426
44116CB00010B/1833